Security and
Public Health

Security and Public Health

Pandemics and Politics in the Contemporary World

Simon Rushton

polity

First published in 2019 by Polity Press

Polity Press
65 Bridge Street
Cambridge CB2 1UR, UK

Polity Press
101 Station Landing
Suite 300
Medford, MA 02155, USA

ISBN-13: 978-1-5095-1588-2
ISBN-13: 978-1-5095-1589-9(pb)

A catalogue record for this book is available from the British Library.

Library of Congress Cataloging-in-Publication Data

Names: Rushton, Simon, 1978- author.
Title: Security and public health : pandemics and politics in the contemporary world / Simon Rushton.
Description: Cambridge, UK ; Medford, MA : Polity, 2019. | Includes bibliographical references and index.
Identifiers: LCCN 2018050591 (print) | LCCN 2018053158 (ebook) | ISBN 9781509515929 (Epub) | ISBN 9781509515882 (hardback) | ISBN 9781509515899 (pb)
Subjects: | MESH: Pandemics–prevention & control | Communicable Disease Control | Politics | Global Health
Classification: LCC RA566.27 (ebook) | LCC RA566.27 (print) | NLM WA 110 | DDC 362.1969/8–dc23
LC record available at https://lccn.loc.gov/2018050591

Typeset in 11 on 13 pt Sabon
by Toppan Best-set Premedia Limited
Printed and bound in Great Britain by TJ International Limited

Contents

Acknowledgements

In thinking about the politics of health security, I have benefitted hugely from the knowledge, insights, ideas and support of a number of friends and colleagues. I owe particular debts of gratitude for countless conversations and their inspiring work over many years to Emma-Louise Anderson, Garrett Wallace Brown, Sara Davies, Alexia Duten, Stefan Elbe, Christian Enemark, Adam Ferhani, Pieter Fourie, Sophie Harman, David Heymann, Steven Hoffman, Alison Howell, Yanzhong Huang, Adam Kamradt-Scott, Maria Kett, Sonja Kittelsen, Kelley Lee, Catherine Yuk-ping Lo, Chris Long, Colin McInnes, João Nunes, Colleen O'Manique, Gorik Ooms, Amy Patterson, Andrew Price-Smith, David Reubi, Stephen Roberts, Anne Roemer-Mahler, Adam Schiller, Jeremy Shiffman, Frank Smith III, Michael Stevenson, Preslava Stoeva, Nick Thomas, Rachel Thompson, Remco van de Pas, Clare Wenham, Owain Williams and Jeremy Youde. I am indebted to all of them – and to all of the others who I embarrassingly forgot to include in the list.

I have also been privileged to be part of some of the most interesting and most nurturing groups of scholars, including the Global Health groups of the International Studies Association, the British International Studies Association and the European International Studies Association, as well as the Centre on Global Health Security at Chatham House. Long may they prosper.

Thanks to the editorial team at Polity Press, especially Louise Knight, Sophie Wright and Nekane Tanaka Galdos, for their support and their patience.

Most of all, I would like to thank all of the students in the Department of Politics at the University of Sheffield who have taken my module *Pandemics and Panics: Health, Security and Global Politics* since it first ran in 2013. I have learned a lot from my conversations with them, and many of the hard questions and interesting cases that we've worked through together have found a home in these pages. This book is dedicated to them.

Introduction: Disease and Security in Historical Perspective

This is a book in defence of politics – a word that often has only negative connotations. Practitioners and policy-makers in medicine and public health frequently see 'politics' as an obstacle that needs to be circumvented. They bemoan the fact that politics gets in the way of attempts to tackle global health crises: governments either have other interests that they choose to prioritize over health (e.g. Hooker et al. 2014), or lack the necessary 'political will' to take decisive action (e.g. Foege 2000). Because of politics, governments fail to cooperate internationally to prevent, detect and control outbreaks (e.g. Kluge et al. 2018). Politics, we often hear, distorts efforts to make health policies truly evidence-based (e.g. Florin 1996). All of these complaints are often true. So why defend politics? In this book, my argument is that politics can be a problem, but it is not *only* a problem – and not inevitably so. Although the ideal for many is to exclude politics from the health policy process, instead moving forward by 'finding out what works' and then 'getting it into policy and practice' (Barnes and Parkhurst 2014: 159), it is only through politics that the deficiencies with current responses to disease crises can be challenged and rectified. Our current failure to adequately protect populations from disease makes politics *more* important, not less. Only by engaging with politics, not turning away from it, can progress be made.

One of the causes of these varying views of the value of politics is differences in what we mean by the term. If we understand politics in a narrow sense, as the activities of governments and other agencies of the state, then current failures are indeed products, to a great extent, of politics. More expansive and critically-oriented definitions of politics, however, are less top-down in nature, focusing instead on the variety of ways in which power structures relationships and seeing a wide variety of actors as able to exercise power through engaging in political acts of various kinds (Bambra, Fox and Scott-Samuel 2005: 190). It is this more expansive view of politics that allows for politics to be a route to change, and that sees politics as a potentially productive rather than merely a restrictive force.

Security, my focus in this book, is a particular kind of politics, but it does not exist in a separate universe to other political considerations. Security policy is often seen as a particularly top-down manifestation of politics – although in this book I will also show the centrality of 'bottom-up' politics to resisting some of the downsides of a security-driven approach to infectious disease, and the role that scientists and other experts not normally thought of as political actors have played in getting disease onto security agendas.

In the field that has come to call itself 'global health', we have spent almost two decades debating whether or not diseases should be viewed as threats to national and international security. Attention has focused on whether 'playing the security card' is a good political strategy, making it more likely that high-level political attention and serious resources will be devoted to tackling global health problems, or whether securitization is dangerous, generating authoritarian and emergency-driven responses that fail to tackle the underlying causes of vulnerability (Elbe 2011).

All of these arguments are covered in this book, but my starting point is that the securitization ship has already sailed. Most Western governments now have infectious diseases well-established on their security policy agendas, with ministries of defence and homeland security, as well as intelligence agencies, working alongside ministries of health to detect, track and respond to outbreaks. What is more, this can no longer be dismissed as solely a preoccupation of developed countries, although it is in the Global North that it is most firmly rooted. The World Health Organization (WHO) routinely talks about 'global health security'. The US-led Global Health Security Agenda has (as of May 2018) 65 member countries drawn from every region of the world. The salient questions now are not whether diseases should or should not be securitized, but rather how, *politically*, security-driven objectives can be reconciled with other important and desirable goals so that we can avoid the downsides of securitization, whilst capturing its upsides. My aim in this book is to move away from what have often been binary discussions over whether or not disease should be securitized towards a discussion of some other, more nuanced, questions:

1. 'How much' security do we feel we need from infectious disease threats, given that in a globalized world we can never be 100% secure?
2. What are we prepared to sacrifice to get the level of security from disease that we desire? Are we willing to bear substantial economic costs? Are we willing to give up some rights and freedoms? Where else might we need to make trade-offs?

Clearly these are questions that will attract a wide range of answers, differing between individuals and between cultures and societies. Government policies may or may not reflect the collective views of their citizens on such questions. Here, I seek to add to current accounts of the contemporary politics of health security by investigating the ways in which policymakers attempt to strike balances between responding to perceived security threats and protecting other values and interests. While being alert to the dangers of securitization, I show in the chapters that follow that securitization does not always produce undesirable outcomes, and that a pragmatic approach is needed to 'understand when security is good or bad in a particular situation' (Nyman 2016: 832). In some of the cases that I examine in this book, I argue that policymakers have got the balance wrong – going too far, or not far enough, to protect us from disease. Sometimes, security-driven actions have even increased insecurity. Elsewhere, however, securitization does appear to have delivered some tangible benefits. Such judgements are inherently political, inviting contestation over how we *do* and how we *should* respond to infectious diseases. Through such debates, politics can be productive. We have no better way of moving towards the right answers than engaging in debate over them.

Some securitization theorists might be sceptical of this view of the politics of security policymaking. According to the classic 'Copenhagen School' framework of securitization (Buzan, Waever and de Wilde 1998), establishing something as a national security threat lifts it 'above' politics, enabling policymakers to break free of the rules of political process that would otherwise bind. In the chapters that follow, I challenge this idea. I argue that in practice we see governments attempting (sometimes successfully, sometimes not) to strike a balance between security and their other perceived interests. The ways in which these balances come to be struck (for better or worse) are deeply political. I show that security considerations do not always determine the outcome of particular policy debates, and that security-driven responses have been successfully challenged through opposition both within and outside formal political processes.

In contrast to much work in the tradition of the Copenhagen School, this entails refuting the idea that securitization is a binary condition in which a particular threat either is or is not securitized, and which assumes that where securitization is successful, security will trump 'mere politics'. Instead, I treat 'security' and 'normal politics' as two ends of a spectrum, with particular threat perceptions and policy responses, such as those examined in this book, more commonly existing at some point between those two extremes (Abrahamsen 2005; McInnes and Rushton 2013). The question that the book poses in terms of securitization is not, therefore, whether or not security logics now dictate responses to infectious diseases, but rather:

3. What are the conditions under which security logics prevail, and when might other (non-security) interests and objectives determine policy outcomes instead?

Although the majority of this book focuses on the contemporary politics of disease and security, in this introductory chapter I set those discussions in their historical context – and in doing so highlight a number of themes that continue to be central to contemporary policy debates around how we secure populations from disease, how far we should go in attempting to do so, and what sacrifices we are prepared to make in pursuit of greater 'health security'.

Disease, History and International Relations

International Relations scholars were surprisingly late in coming to recognize the global politics of disease. I say this is surprising because, as is examined in the following sections of this chapter, infectious diseases have been threats that all societies through history have faced, and governments have long sought to put in place measures to protect populations from their devastating impacts. It is also true that the global nature of contagion – and the need to act internationally to successfully control the cross-border spread of disease – was recognized long ago, at least a century before the creation of the World Health Organization which now attempts to live up to the task of coordinating international efforts to prevent and control outbreaks. Pathogens, then, were a source of insecurity long before International Relations scholars began to study them, even if they were less commonly spoken of by policymakers in explicitly 'security' terms.

It was only from the turn of the millennium that International Relations began to pay real attention to the relationship between disease and national and international security. Andrew Price-Smith (2001), Stefan Elbe (2003), David Fidler (2003a, 2003b), Kelley Lee and Colin McInnes (2003) and Christian Enemark (2005), amongst others, made particularly noteworthy early interventions in the field. Gradually, research on the global politics of disease has moved from the extreme periphery of the discipline to, if still not exactly central, at least occupying a recognized place within it. University courses with titles like 'Contemporary Security Challenges' now routinely include consideration of disease. Mainstream security textbooks feature chapters on it.

This has been an area in which epidemiological events, policymaking and academic analysis have developed alongside one another. The UN Security Council's discussions on AIDS in 2000, at a time of widely proclaimed crisis in the development of the pandemic, were a key moment both in illustrating to policymakers that disease could (and some thought should) have a place on security policy agendas, but also in convincing scholars that the concepts and tools of International Relations could profitably be brought to bear on health issues. It was natural, then, that much of the early scholarship focused on AIDS, and then on a series of subsequent disease crises that were explicitly dealt with by governments in security terms, from Severe Acute Respiratory Syndrome (SARS) to H5N1 ('bird flu') to H1N1 ('swine flu') to Ebola.

Because it has become more prominent on the agendas of security policy actors in recent years, there has often been a tendency to see disease as a *new security challenge* – something that came onto the scene only once the Cold

War was safely behind us and policymakers began to take a broader view of threats to national security. There is some truth in this. But saying that something is (relatively) new on mainstream security policy agendas is not the same as saying that the threat itself is new. In the remainder of this chapter, I discuss the fact that disease is one of the oldest threats that societies have faced, and argue that it is important to engage with that social, political and economic history of disease, both the continuities and the discontinuities, to gain an understanding of contemporary policy dilemmas and approaches. First, I discuss the fact that societies have always been challenged by disease threats and that over time they have developed new ways of responding to disease that have been driven not only by scientific progress but also by political developments. Second, I argue that providing citizens with some degree of protection against disease (in other words, of viewing disease as a threat to be defended against, rather than an inevitable and unavoidable fact of life) has not just been 'on the agenda' of governments, but has been fundamental to the development of ideas about what government is *for*. The emergence of the modern state has gone hand-in-hand with its attempts to provide for public health, and populations have increasingly come to seek and expect protection against 'invading' microbes. Third, I show how the construction of, and action on, disease threats has long had an international dimension. Disease has often been associated with the threat posed by the 'other' beyond our borders, and states (especially European states) have historically engaged in international cooperation on cross-border disease control in order to keep themselves safe. To declare, as the UK government did in 2011 (HM Government 2011), that 'Health is Global' was a statement of long-standing historical fact, not a claim about a new twenty-first-century reality.

All of this illustrates the fact that, whilst infectious disease is a relatively new concern of academic International Relations, it is not a new concern for those engaged in the conduct of international relations. Legacies of colonial-era health and 'tropical medicine', and of almost two centuries of regular diplomatic engagement on disease control, show that, in various ways, disease has long been an international political issue. The contemporary policy questions and dilemmas with which this book is primarily concerned have roots that stretch far back into that history.

Disease, Politics and Scientific Progress

Short of living in a hermetically sealed bubble, humans can never be entirely safe from the threat of infection. The same is true of nations: whilst in theory a state could seal its borders and dramatically reduce the chances of an infectious disease not already present from entering, in reality no country in the modern world is able to achieve this level of isolation – and even if it could, the downsides would almost certainly outweigh the benefits. Discussions of the transnational nature of contemporary infectious disease threats frequently revolve around globalization (Cockerham and Cockerham 2010; McMurray and Smith 2001), but whilst globalization-related changes have no doubt sped up the movement of pathogens around the world, such movement was always a reality of life on earth. For thousands of years, societies have been impacted by outbreaks of infectious disease originating beyond their borders, and for thousands of years they have sought to mitigate their effects (Hays 2009).

In his 2009 book *Contagion and Chaos*, Andrew Price-Smith (2009: chapter 2) provided a compelling historical account of the various ways in which infectious disease has acted as a 'stressor' on societies. Examining a series of epidemics over the course of recorded history, Price-Smith showed that pathogens have challenged societies in ways that go far beyond the obvious effects of morbidity and mortality. These challenges have included inducing political and social instability (in extreme cases even contributing to the collapse of entire civilizations, as with the Amerindian societies devastated by smallpox), causing migration as people attempt to 'get out of harm's way', undermining economies, and playing a part in determining the course of armed conflicts.

As Price-Smith also notes, as well as posing direct challenges to social, economic and political stability, epidemics have often exacerbated underlying social tensions, with particular ethnic groups or social classes, for example, being blamed for the introduction of a disease into a population. As will be discussed later in this book, the politics of blame remains a potent feature of contemporary disease politics, with certain groups either explicitly or implicitly being seen as posing a risk to the rest of us. In some cases, such blaming reflects a genuinely increased likelihood of infection amongst certain groups (although whether this makes those people 'perpetrators', 'victims' or something else is a highly politicized question); in others, blaming tells us far more about societal prejudices than about epidemiology.

Our collective cultural memories of disease also deeply condition the ways in which we see and interpret new and future pathogenic threats. The 'Spanish' influenza outbreak which followed the First World War, for example, has become a touchstone for discussions of current and potential future influenza pandemics. The 'swine flu' pandemic of 2009 (discussed in chapter 1) came to be written off as mild in comparison to Spanish flu, whilst the potential that a new mutation of the influenza virus could lead to the emergence of a strain as deadly as Spanish flu raises concerns about future security risks, generating terrifying epidemiological projections and huge estimates of potential global mortality. The plague has similarly become a potent cultural marker of death and destruction, especially in European societies. Susan Sontag noted that AIDS in the 1980s was often discussed through the metaphor of plague (Sontag 1989). The same metaphor has been deployed in relation to a huge range of other social and political challenges, from drug abuse (Reinarman and Levine 1989) to Soviet communism (Hoover 2011: section 1). Our collective understandings of historical disease outbreaks condition how we view the world – not least how we respond to contemporary disease threats, calculate future risks and prepare to face them. As João Nunes (2014: 83) has aptly put it, 'historical examples of death and turmoil caused by disease function as repositories of meaning for interpreting present outbreaks.'

Improvements over time in knowledge and understanding about the causes of disease have, naturally, profoundly shaped the ways in which societies have sought to defend themselves. New developments continue to do so. And although it is tempting to view ourselves as living close to the pinnacle of scientific and medical advancement, it seems certain that our descendants in centuries to come will look back on the twenty-first century as an era in which understanding was limited (and in some cases wrong) and a time when attempts to protect individuals and societies from infectious diseases were unimaginably, perhaps even laughably, primitive. It is certainly common enough for us to look back on earlier historical periods in just such a way. The carrying of posies to ward off disease or the belief that tobacco offers protection against infection seem to us to be hopelessly misguided efforts at preventing illness. Perhaps more surprising, though, is the extent to which previous generations adopted response measures that *were* relatively effective, despite a lack of accurate scientific knowledge about the underlying causes of disease. Many of our contemporary methods of responding to outbreaks have long historical antecedents. The development of quarantine – a measure still frequently used to control the spread of infection – is generally traced back to the 1300s (Tognotti, 2013), long before germs or viruses were known to cause disease. Centuries later, John Snow, seen by many as the father of the science of epidemiology, succeeded in persuading the authorities to put in place an effective 'policy response' – the removal of the Broad Street pump handle, which, according to the standard, although unfortunately partly apocryphal account (McLeod 2000; Paneth 2004) brought to an end a major cholera outbreak in Soho, London in 1854 – without any detailed understanding of the *Vibro cholerae* bacteria that cause the disease.

Over time, the germ theory of disease and many other scientific discoveries have incrementally improved societies' ability to prevent and contain outbreaks, and to cure the sick. It is central to the approach adopted in this book, however, that even 'technical' public health interventions are profoundly and unavoidably political, being tightly bound up with prevailing power structures as well as societal norms, rules and institutions. Political changes, as well as breakthroughs in science and medicine, have affected the options available to policymakers seeking to respond to disease outbreaks, and the acceptability of certain kinds of interventions has varied over time.

The practice of 'shutting up' houses during the London plague of 1665 is one example of the ways in which public health ethics have shifted in tandem with wider social norms, in turn changing understandings of the legitimate exercise of power. Shutting up – discussed by Samuel Pepys and Daniel Defoe, amongst others (McKinlay 2009) – was carried out on houses in which a resident had died of plague. Those living in the house, even those who were asymptomatic, were forcibly confined to the premises, with the doors being padlocked and watchmen stationed outside to prevent escape, as a means of protecting the wider community against the threat of contagion. Such policies, which effectively imprisoned those guilty of no crime and involved knowingly incarcerating the healthy alongside those thought likely to be contagious, are difficult to reconcile with modern ideas of medical ethics and human rights. But even here we can find historical continuities. Just as the plague itself remains a touchstone for modern political debates, policies such as shutting up continue to provide the background to contemporary discussions of epidemic response. At the time of the 2009–10 H1N1 'swine flu' outbreak, the journal *Public Health Ethics* reproduced an anonymous 1665 pamphlet on the ethics of shutting up (Anonymous 2010), arguing that 'it is interesting to see that the seven arguments that are advanced against compulsory isolation [in the pamphlet] are, mostly, as relevant today as they were in 1665' (Verweij and Dawson 2010: 1–2). The points made by the anonymous pamphleteer in the seventeenth century were indeed strikingly similar to some of those seen in contemporary debates over quarantine, including arguments focusing on the threat to human dignity (which might now be couched in terms of human rights or civil liberties), its effectiveness as a method of disease control, and the unintended consequences of such restrictive measures. Here we see the history of disease control efforts directly informing discussions which bring together medico-scientific evidence and political considerations in determining what types of policy response to disease outbreaks are and are not ethically acceptable – a key theme of subsequent chapters.

A related issue that will recur throughout the book is that medical and scientific developments do not always make us safer from disease, and even when they do, they often raise new political questions to which the answers are not always simple. Most medics and medical researchers would no doubt want to argue that the history of medicine is overwhelmingly a history of discoveries that have improved human health and wellbeing. Comparing contemporary life expectancies (especially in developed countries) or contemporary child survival statistics with those of past centuries makes the point powerfully. Yet scientific progress is not a one-way street. Some scientific developments have opened up new forms of risk – as we will see in chapter 3 with recent breakthroughs in synthetic biology that raise the possibility of new and more deadly pathogens being deliberately created. Even where the positive health benefits of scientific research have been more uncontroversial, hugely politicized questions have arisen. Amongst others, we have seen this in debates over the appropriate focus of research efforts and the distribution of the resulting benefits. The identification of a category of 'Neglected Tropical Diseases' (NTDs) was based on the realization that certain diseases suffer from severe underinvestment in terms of pharmaceutical research and development – particularly those diseases that primarily affect poor populations in the Global South, who represent a relatively unattractive market for private pharmaceutical firms (Hotez 2008). In some cases where new drugs have been developed, there have been lengthy struggles over their affordability, most famously seen in the activism of the late 1990s and early 2000s that sought to establish the right of poor people living with HIV and AIDS to have access to antiretroviral therapies (Chan 2015: chapter 3). The (relatively) rich and powerful – or those, such as militaries, deemed to be strategically important – have usually been the first to benefit from new medical and scientific advances. Yet, as is discussed in the next section, the poor have sometimes benefitted too. Disease has transformed the relationship between governors and governed. Indeed, protection of the population from illness, to make them healthy and productive citizens, has become integral to the very *raison d'être* of the modern nation state.

Disease, the Individual and the State

As someone profoundly interested in the historical development of the relationship between states and their citizens, Michel Foucault devoted considerable energy to understanding the ways in which health and medicine have impacted upon those relationships. He identified the eighteenth century as a turning point – an era that (in Western European states, at least) 'saw the multiplication of doctors, the foundation of new hospitals, the opening of free health clinics, and, in a general fashion, an increased consumption of treatment in every class of society' (Foucault 2014: 114). Crucially, however, Foucault traced the effects of these developments far beyond medical facilities and individual doctor–patient relationships, noting an

at least partial integration of medical practice with economic and political managements, which aimed at the rationalization of society. Medicine was no longer simply an important technique in the lives and deaths of individuals about which the collectivities were never indifferent; it became, in the framework of group decisions, an essential element for the maintenance and development of the collectivity. (Foucault 2014: 114)

For Foucault, then, medicine served an important function in establishing and strengthening collective (national) identities. Priscilla Wald (2008: 51) argues much the same thing about modern narratives of disease in which 'The depiction of contagion offers a visceral way to imagine communal affiliation in national terms.' The result of emerging governmental interest in health and disease within the population, according to Foucault, was a range of new government priorities around surveillance, continually measuring and collecting health data, and putting in place preventive measures – sometimes seen as paternalistic or even authoritarian interventions – to improve public health. New forms of state bureaucracy emerged to fulfil these functions.

Infectious diseases such as plague, leprosy and cholera were particularly important in this developing state role in protecting (and at the same time seeking to exert control over) populations. In part this was simply a reflection of the most pressing health challenges facing those societies at that time. For most of human history, infectious diseases have been the primary cause of premature death and serious illness. For most of the developed world this is no longer the case, with non-communicable diseases (NCDs) (sometimes popularly, but problematically, characterized as 'lifestyle diseases') now representing the primary disease burden in comparatively wealthier societies. US Surgeon-General William H. Stewart is remembered for having (supposedly) declared in the late 1960s that 'It is time to close the book on infectious diseases, and declare the war against pestilence won.' Whilst there is room for doubt about whether Stewart ever in fact said such a thing (Spellberg and Taylor-Blake 2013), the quote is taken by many to be representative of a more general feeling in the mid-twentieth century that the era of infectious diseases as a major cause of death in the developed world was over. This claim has been roundly mocked by subsequent commentators, especially given the rise of antibiotic resistance and the contemporary prominence of 'Emerging Infectious Diseases' (EIDs) in public health policy discourse, discussed in detail in the next chapter (see also Lakoff and Collier 2008: 9; Weir and Mykhalovskiy 2010). Yet the over-exaggeration hides a broader truth about epidemiological transition in the developed world in which infectious diseases now rank lowly in the list of routine population health threats as compared with risk factors such as obesity, smoking and the consumption of alcohol (GBD 2015 Mortality and Causes of Death Collaborators 2016). Even in the Global South, where infectious diseases still account for a relatively high percentage of the total disease burden, a notable shift is under way in which non-communicable diseases are moving up the league tables of causes of death (see chapter 6).

But the fact that infectious diseases were (and in many places still are) a major cause of sickness and death is not the sole reason for their historical prominence on government agendas. Some of the other reasons for this prioritization, indeed, are important in helping us to explain the continuing privileging of communicable over non-communicable diseases in contemporary global health governance (Youde 2012: 160). First, contagion is a process that by its very nature generates fear within populations, and consequently also within governments. The spread of a disease, especially a deadly one, through a community inevitably creates intense concern amongst citizens, media and government. Better surveillance data and improved knowledge about the transmission of diseases may make modern societies even more prone to such 'pandemic anxiety' (Ingram 2008). Second, the cross-border movement of pathogens adds a further dimension to this fear of contagion, invoking comparisons with a military invasion, and frequently leading to the linking of disease importation with other security concerns, including migration and border security (Coker and Ingram 2006). Third, infectious diseases often affect those who, historically, have mattered most to a state: young men who are economically productive and are needed to serve in the military. For most of history, health threats to women, such as unsafe childbirth, have, frankly, mattered little to the state. The same is true of illnesses that primarily affect the elderly. Fourth, the very fact that infectious diseases are now a less common cause of death in the developed world than non-communicable diseases seems to have brought a greater degree of sensitivity to such 'unusual' forms of threat, creating the sense of impending crisis seen in the public discourse over many of the cases examined in this book, from SARS to Ebola. Finally, over time there has been an increasing emphasis not only on the direct impact of disease on society in terms of illness and death, but also the spillover effects such as economic losses and societal disruption.[1] In short, there are a range of persuasive reasons why governments have interpreted infectious disease threats in particular (security-laden) ways, and why they have wanted to put in place measures to provide their populations with protection.

If political and security concerns have made governments take notice of infectious diseases, they have also affected their responses. Power and ideology have profoundly shaped the ways in which governments have interpreted and addressed disease threats within and beyond their borders. To take one example, the fact that the biomedical model came to dominate health policymaking in the twentieth century has been seen as having narrowed the terms of the debate. As Priscilla Wald notes in her discussion of Laurie Garrett's seminal *The Coming Plague* (Garrett 1994), a book that played an important part in convincing the Clinton administration of the threat to the US posed by infectious diseases, 'The familiar story she ... summons – the outbreak narrative – shifts the terms of her analysis of global health. Microbial warfare directs attention to the microbes and thereby presents the threat of disease emergence in predominantly medical terms' (Wald 2008: 267). As we will see in chapters 5 and 6, getting lost in such a medicalized account are the deeper structural factors that determine health outcomes – not least the scourge of poverty (Farmer 1999; Hays 2009: chapter 12). The 'pro-health politics' that I make a case for in the Conclusion to this book, following this line of thought, is not a narrow medico-pharmaceutical 'war' against microbes (or, at least, not only that), but rather one that embraces critical public health's traditional strengths of identifying and seeking to tackle the underlying political, social and economic determinants of poor health, not least national and global inequalities. Too often, as I show in the chapters that follow, the primary interest of powerful states has been in combatting individual 'threatening' microbes rather than grappling with the deeper structural causes of health insecurity.

The Threat of the 'Other' and the Need for International Responses

The twentieth century and the advent of the biomedical approach did not create this defensive dynamic *de novo*. Rather, biomedicine combined with pre-existing ideas about disease and insecurity *and* with a long history of thinking about threats posed by the 'other' residing beyond our borders. For centuries, fears of 'new' or 'foreign' diseases have been closely bound up with fears of other peoples – especially those seen as 'primitive' – and, thus, with a wider politics of race, colonization and domination. Here, too, we find continuities.

The origins of the modern discipline of global public health can be traced back to colonial-era 'tropical medicine' (Aginam 2003). Whilst tropical medicine was, on the face of it at least, concerned with dividing the world climatically, between the 'tropics' and the temperate climates of Western Europe and North America, it frequently slipped into ideas that seem jarring to modern ears, including tropes about unhygienic lifestyles and primitive cultural practices in the (colonized) tropics and the superiority of (white, Western) medical knowledge and technologies. As Alison Bashford (2004) has noted, tropical medicine became not only about health narrowly defined, but part of the prevailing 'systems and cultures of race management' designed to segregate the safe spaces of the colonizer from the dangerous colonized through *cordons sanitaires* and other public health-framed policy interventions.

It would be surprising to see such explicitly racialized ideas in contemporary global health discourse, but some are beginning to question whether contemporary global health itself is in some respects neocolonialist (Horton 2013). Certainly, as we will see in later chapters, it is possible to discern striking similarities between tropical medicine ideas of the nineteenth century and some of the underpinning assumptions detectable in discussions of (global) health security in the present day. For Obijofor Aginam (2003), attempts to 'insulate' Europe from the diseases of the barbarous 'other' remain readily discernible in contemporary global health governance in which, despite the rhetoric of shared risk in a globalized world (see chapter 5), 'over 3.3 billion people in the world are banished to the penitentiary of health insecurity'. Along the same lines, Gregory Bankoff finds in current discussions of Western vulnerability to disease a continuation of a historical discourse which

> denigrates large regions of the world as dangerous – disease-ridden, poverty-stricken and disaster-prone; one that depicts the inhabitants of these regions as inferior – untutored, incapable, victims; and that it reposes in Western medicine, investment and preventive systems the expertise required to remedy these ills. (Bankoff 2001: 29)

The earliest international efforts by governments to develop cooperative mechanisms to mitigate the risks posed by the transnational spread of disease, not coincidentally, came about during the colonial era. International cooperation on disease control is most commonly traced back to the International Sanitary Conferences of the mid-nineteenth century, which brought together European states concerned with harmonizing quarantine regulations in order to control cholera, plague and yellow fever. David Fidler (2001) identifies the 1851–1881 International Sanitary Conferences as the birth of what has now come to be known as 'global health diplomacy', with each of the countries taking part in the conferences being represented by a diplomat and a physician (Howard-Jones 1975: 12), an early glimpse of what has in recent years become a far more routine cooperation between the worlds of public health/medicine and foreign policy (Elbe 2010). Some of the themes identified in the preceding discussions – including scientific debates over the aetiology of cholera – were major features of these nineteenth-century conferences, with progress on international action being stymied by unreconciled differences in opinion over the cause of transmission (Hoffman 2010; Howard-Jones 1975). Whilst that uncertainty disappeared as a result of subsequent scientific advances, the historical continuities between nineteenth-century multilateral disease control efforts and those of the present day are in some ways more striking than the discontinuities.

One such continuity is the wish of governments to balance disease control with their desire to keep international trade moving. The Conferences of the nineteenth century involved the major (primarily European) maritime powers of the day, with the first International Sanitary Convention, finally agreed in 1892 at the seventh in the series of conferences, being focused on harmonizing quarantine arrangements for ships passing through the Suez Canal. The gradual institutionalization of these international arrangements (Hoffman 2010) led ultimately to the adoption of the International Sanitary Regulations by the new WHO in 1951 (WHA 1951). These were revised in 1969 and again in 2005 when WHO member states adopted a new set of International Health Regulations (IHR), which remain in force at the time of writing. Although the scope of international disease control efforts had broadened significantly through these successive sets of regulations, the purpose and scope of the 2005 IHR, as set out in Article 2 – 'to prevent, protect against, control and provide a public health response to the international spread of disease in ways that are commensurate with and restricted to public health risks, and which avoid unnecessary interference with international traffic and trade' (WHO 2016: 10) – would have been readily recognizable to participants in the International Sanitary Conferences of 150 years ago. Whilst, as we will see in chapter 1, it is common to appeal to concepts such as 'globalization' and to technological developments such as the advent of air travel to highlight the newness of infectious disease as a security threat, the idea that increasing international interconnectedness posed new risks of disease importation was already well established in the mid-nineteenth century (Huber 2006). Rather than air travel, it was steamships and railways that were then seen to be speeding up the rate at which diseases travelled from place to place. The underlying perception of the threat, however, was the same. What is more, the desire of governments at the time was not to respond by restricting the new steam-powered methods of travel and trade – quite the reverse. They wanted to develop ways to reduce disease risks (accepting they could not be reduced to zero) *without* disrupting cross-border trade. Here we can clearly see evidence of one of the core claims of this book: that the attempts by governments to provide security from disease are not (and never have been) on the basis of 'security at all costs'. Rather, protection from disease is always balanced against other interests – in the case of the International Sanitary Conventions and the current International Health Regulations, primarily against the economic costs associated with disrupting the global political economy.

Chapter Outline

This book examines the contemporary politics of security and public health both 'vertically' and 'horizontally', focusing on specific disease threats in the first three chapters, and cross-cutting issues in chapters 4–6. Chapters 1–3 each look at one of the disease-related threats that have become most firmly established on national and international security agendas: rapidly-spreading pandemics of deadly diseases; HIV and AIDS; and the threat posed by man-made outbreaks, either deliberate or inadvertent. These three sources of perceived threat have been chosen because they allow us to examine the very different ways in which disease has been framed as a security problem, and the variety of forms of mitigation that governments have sought to use to reduce the risk.

Chapter 1 examines rapidly-spreading pandemic diseases. I show how these came increasingly to be seen by states in security terms, with public health and medical experts playing important roles in convincing security policymakers that pathogens, especially 'Emerging Infectious Diseases', constituted a threat to national and international security in a globalized world. Pandemics, they argued, endangered not only the lives and wellbeing of populations, but also threatened to wreak economic and social havoc – a problem that they saw as more acute than ever before in the modern global village. Advocates for 'Global Health Security' were clear that international cooperation would be vital to detect and control outbreaks quickly, limiting the spread. But that cooperation would not be pursued on the basis of security at all costs, but rather in ways that sought to mitigate transnational disease threats whilst minimizing the impact on international travel and trade. The long-term success of global cooperation, it was argued, would depend on countries not being 'punished' for experiencing outbreaks by having unnecessary travel and trade restrictions placed on them. Although security communities came to rhetorically accept this logic, during emergencies what governments see as being good for national security is often in tension with what is best for longer-term cooperation (and, ultimately, for global health security). The chapter looks at this tension by examining the ways in which governments have used border controls during outbreak emergencies, including the 2014–16 West African Ebola outbreak. It argues that governments often prioritize their short-term security interests over the proper functioning of the 'global health security regime', threatening to create bigger problems in the longer term if international cooperation is undermined. Reconciling these short- and long-term interests, I argue, will need determined international political engagement between emergencies, rather than during them.

In chapter 2, the focus is on HIV and AIDS – a case that has been seen by many International Relations scholars as a perfect example of a successful securitization process. The chapter begins by tracing how AIDS came to be linked to security, particularly the role that some feared it would play in further weakening what were already seen as 'fragile states' in sub-Saharan Africa. The acceptance of this link by policy elites coincided with a huge surge in international attention and resources for AIDS, including the provision of medication on a far larger scale and attempts to promote behaviour change with the aim of slowing and reversing the pandemic and reducing its social, political and economic impacts. Some critics were rightly concerned that framing AIDS as a security threat could have the side-effect of making people living with HIV and AIDS (PLWHA) 'threats to the state'. Certainly in the early days of AIDS this was a problem, and discrimination against (and even persecution of) PLWHA has continued at some times and in some places, adding credence to this fear. But overall, the downsides of securitization have not been as acute as some feared. I argue that there a number of reasons why, in the AIDS case, the downsides may have been mitigated. First, security has not been the only game in town: other motives for international action, not least that AIDS was seen as an impediment to international development, mattered too. Second, the interventions that were needed to tackle AIDS were far removed from the short-term emergency measures that have typified responses to faster-moving outbreaks. But finally, and perhaps most importantly, I argue that to understand international action on AIDS we need to look not only at elite-level policy discourses, but also at the vibrant history of advocacy and activism. This was important in bringing about the high political profile of AIDS, as well as helping to reduce some of the feared dangers of securitization, such as discrimination and other abuses of rights. Here we see that security does not necessarily exclude other forms of politics – indeed it can live alongside them, sometimes in mutually-reinforcing ways. The longer-term and more community-oriented approaches that have developed around AIDS may offer a model for thinking about how to respond to other types of global health security threat.

Chapter 3 examines the ways in which science, especially bioscience research, has come to be seen as a new source of security risk. Developments in synthetic biology and related fields have led security policymakers to worry about disease risks emanating from various sources: from the actions of bioterrorists or rogue individuals, from accidental laboratory escapes, or (increasingly) from the unregulated activities of 'amateur', 'hobbyist' scientists. The deliberate modification of pathogens, either as a part of legitimate biological research or ill-intentioned efforts to create a weapon, could lead to widespread and deadly outbreaks arising without warning, and with little in the way of effective defences in place. Although there has been a relatively limited history of man-made disease outbreaks occurring in practice, powerful narratives of future threat have become well established. One of the biggest policy challenges in this area, however, is that the actual level of risk is incredibly difficult to quantify. Calibrating security responses appropriately is therefore a very challenging task. Various policy interventions are possible, including more strongly regulating laboratories and access to equipment, or attempting to control the dissemination of potentially 'dangerous' scientific knowledge. But again the balance is a delicate one: too much intervention and regulation could stymie scientific progress and waste resources; not enough could leave governments open to accusations of having not taken the threat seriously enough.

In chapters 1, 2 and 3, then, we see security concerns being balanced against other perceived interests in very different ways. In chapter 1, the desire is to maximize security whilst minimizing the impact on international trade, and to find ways of reconciling short-term perceptions of national interest with longer-term collective interests. In chapter 2, the desire is to control the virus, which includes attempting to change individual behaviours to prevent those who are already infected from passing the disease on, in a way that is compatible with human rights concerns. In chapter 3, the balance being struck is between minimizing the risks of scientific research without unduly hindering academic freedom and scientific progress. In short, across these three chapters we see security-driven efforts to regulate borders, to regulate individual behaviours, and to regulate science – each of which comes with potential drawbacks.

Chapters 4, 5 and 6 take a 'horizontal' look at the potential problems arising from securitizing disease, and in doing so begin to identify some key elements of what a 'pro-health politics' might look like.

In chapter 4, I examine what security-based responses to disease emergencies can mean for human rights and civil liberties. Unlike in chapter 2, where the AIDS community has been highly influential (and to a great extent successful) in forwarding the case for a rights-based approach, in the case of rapidly-spreading pandemic diseases, the balance between security and rights often ends up being struck in a very different way. In this chapter I examine how this plays out in terms of the treatment of 'suspect' people at borders and quarantine arrangements during outbreaks. Looking at these common forms of outbreak response in relation to the Siracusa Principles, which are supposed to guide governments who seek to derogate from civil and political rights during an emergency, I argue that although they are too often honoured in the breach, those principles do at least give us a yardstick against which to judge policy actions, and a basis on which to oppose emergency responses that are anti-democratic, discriminatory and stigmatizing. Furthermore, in practice the conflict between public health and human rights is not so binary as is often supposed. There are circumstances in which curtailing rights in the name of security might actually lead to *less* public health security, not more. In the final part of the chapter, I look at an alternative way of thinking about this security versus rights dilemma: as a conflict between individual rights and the collective right to health. Although forwarding this as a basis for policymaking is hampered by a lack of clarity over what the right to health entails, and a lack of enthusiasm for such a right amongst many governments, it nonetheless points us to the fact that another politics of disease is possible, and that a genuine 'pro-health politics' must be one that has human rights at its core.

While chapter 4 focuses on individual-level rights, chapter 5 focuses on wider global structures of socio-economic inequality. These inequalities, the chapter argues, are the root causes of many contemporary infectious disease risks. While much of the discourse on global health security presents cross-border infectious disease outbreaks as inevitable and unavoidable in a globalized world, I argue that this is in some ways a problematic assumption. Human actions and political choices have a huge part to play in producing and increasing disease risks: risks that in practice are borne disproportionately by the global poor, even though, paradoxically, it is the richest states and societies who are most prone to seeing diseases as national security threats. Governments often talk about shared global risks, but that risk is shared highly unevenly. Contemporary global efforts designed to address global health security threats focus largely on surveillance to catch outbreaks early, and containment efforts when they emerge. In some cases where containment has failed, the international community has been forced to implement a larger-scale response effort. But these tend to be short-term emergency responses that do little to grapple with the underlying structural problems, and that move on once the crisis has passed, leaving the conditions that produced the outbreak in the first place little improved. If governments (not least governments of the Global North) do want security, it certainly does not look like they are prepared to pursue it 'at all costs'. Approaches that go further than this, that seek to engage in prevention by addressing the socio-economic roots of disease emergence, must be central to a more progressive 'pro-health politics'.

Chapter 6 broadens the discussion still further – beyond infectious diseases – to examine what impact the securitization of particular pathogenic threats has had on the global health agenda as a whole. Here I argue that securitization has had real effects on priorities, and in doing so has created opportunity costs in that the same resources cannot also be used to tackle other health issues. What is more, the everyday health insecurities that the majority of the world faces are nowhere to be seen in the global health security discourse, including non-communicable diseases and even many endemic infectious diseases that are not considered 'security relevant' because they do not cross borders. This prioritization needs to be understood as a political choice. In this chapter I am also interested in showing that other forms of global health politics *do* exist and can also be capable of generating action and resources. Looking at the ways in which health has been approached as an international development issue through processes such as the Millennium Development Goals (MDGs) and the Sustainable Development Goals (SDGs), I show that security is not the only value that matters. But security remains important, not only impacting on priorities for spending but also profoundly affecting how we understand the term 'global health' in the first place. It is not only prioritization that is political: de-prioritization is too, and a narrow understanding of the ways in which health is global can obscure more than it illuminates. A 'pro-health politics' would seek to challenge some of these political choices and to bring the everyday health insecurities that affect the majority of the world's population back into focus.

Given that securitization is now well-entrenched in the global health policy discourse, I argue in the concluding chapter that challenging dominant ideas about what constitutes effective security policy, rather than attempting to unpick securitization itself, may be the best route forward. There is a strong argument to be made that taking the global health security narrative seriously would justify approaches that would incorporate the elements identified in chapters 4, 5 and 6 around rights, prevention and the broadening of the agenda. I argue that the concepts of dignity and solidarity, rarely seen in discussions of health security, could actually be far more effective routes towards embedding these ideas and achieving security for all than exclusion and fear. Achieving this shift in approach would require a determined political engagement – and the development of a genuine 'pro-health politics'. Such a politics would take seriously public health efforts to understand health risks at different scales, from the individual right up to the global, and to engage in preventive measures rather than reactive crisis management. As the best critical public health scholarship does, this would entail a serious engagement with the political, social and economic determinants of health that structure health outcomes for populations around the world. Unfortunately, the tide currently seems to be flowing in the other direction, towards apparently depoliticized evidence-based approaches that fail to challenge the status quo. In response, I argue that health professionals, and also civil society, need to play a part in repoliticization and forwarding the case for a broader and more inclusive vision of health security.

– 1 –

Pandemics and Global Health Security

In early 2009, something unusual was happening in Mexico. A cluster of influenza infections around Veracruz was eventually recognized as something more significant: early cases of a new strain of the influenza virus with pandemic potential. Information in the early stages was scarce. It wasn't clear where the new strain had come from, how easily the virus was transmitting between people, or what the fatality rate was. Initially the death toll in Mexico seemed extremely high, prompting concerns that the next 'big one', comparable to the Spanish flu epidemic that followed the First World War, had arrived.

The new strain of the virus – officially labelled H1N1, but more commonly known as 'swine flu' – quickly spread around the world. The fact that it gradually became clear that the fatality rate was not as high as had originally been assumed eventually calmed fears somewhat. But not before most states had implemented their pandemic preparedness plans, and the WHO had (for the first time ever) declared a 'public health emergency of international concern'.

In the previous chapter, I argued that the idea that infectious diseases represent a threat to national and international security is now well established – and indeed has long historical precedents, even if the language of national and international security was used less frequently in the past. I argued that rather than continuing to debate whether we should or should not securitize disease, we need to pay more attention than we have done so far to three important questions: how much security do we feel we need from disease threats? What are we prepared to sacrifice to achieve that level of security? And, what are the conditions under which security logics prevail in guiding responses to perceived disease threats?

This chapter begins the process of analysing these questions. I focus on pandemics of rapidly-spreading and deadly diseases – perhaps the most obvious, and certainly the most emblematic, of all health security threats. I describe the way in which pathogens, most notably Emerging and Re-emerging Infectious Diseases (ERIDs) and pandemic strains of influenza (pandemic flu), came to be widely accepted as national and international security concerns, particularly amongst governments in the Global North. I discuss the international mechanisms that are supposed to mitigate the effects of such crises and how they seek to balance states' security and trade interests. However, as I discuss in the second part of the chapter, national and international security can be in tension with one another – especially in the emergency conditions of a major health emergency. Examining border closures as a common policy response, I show that in many cases we have seen governments facing a perceived crisis prioritizing their own national security and ignoring their obligations within the international cooperative arrangements that are supposed to provide for what has come to be known as 'global health security'. Are these tensions inevitable during an emergency? If so, why don't all governments act in this way? And is it possible, politically, to move towards achieving security from pandemics in a way that incorporates a greater degree of international solidarity?

Epidemics and Pandemics

The terms 'epidemic' and 'pandemic' are often used interchangeably in the statements of policymakers, and also in the wider public discourse. To some extent the difference is academic given that both can be understood as posing security threats to populations and the state. Yet the distinction between the two terms does guide our attention towards important issues of scale and territory. The sixth edition of A Dictionary of Epidemiology (Porta 2014) defines an epidemic as 'The occurrence in a community or region of cases of an illness, specific health-related behavior, or other health-related events clearly in excess of normal expectancy.' The crucial difference here is between that which would normally be expected (in epidemiological terms, diseases that are 'endemic') in a particular population, and something unusual, new or unexpected. A pandemic, meanwhile, is defined as 'An epidemic occurring over a very wide area, crossing international boundaries, and usually affecting a large number of people.' The key differences between an epidemic and a pandemic, therefore, are of scale (the number of people infected) and territory (the geographical area affected).

In technical public health terms, the words epidemic and pandemic tell us only about epidemiology; about how far and to whom a disease has spread. They tell us nothing about the severity of the disease. The Dictionary of Epidemiology's definition of pandemic, indeed, goes on to warn the reader that 'Only some pandemics cause severe disease in some individuals or at a population level' (Porta 2014).

Such technical definitions, however, only get us so far. Beyond the world of professional epidemiologists, 'epidemic' and 'pandemic' are powerful words that can have significant effects. As Sander L. Gilman wrote in The Lancet, reflecting on the H1N1 'swine flu' pandemic of 2009:

> 'epidemic' maintains a powerful metaphorical connection to universal, lethal contagion from its earliest to its most recent use. Epidemic and pandemic have a strong metaphorical use in terms of the unfettered spread of deadly and uncontrolled diseases and have always had social and emotional consequences. (Gilman 2010: 1866)

To this, we might add that the use of these terms can also have significant political and economic effects. Policy-makers are, of course, acutely aware of this. In dealing with swine flu, even the WHO, often seen as a highly technical agency, showed full cognizance of the political and economic consequences of labelling the outbreak a pandemic. In the early stages, indeed, the organization resisted officially declaring a pandemic. According to the WHO's official updates, by 21 May 2009, laboratory-confirmed cases of H1N1 influenza had been reported by forty-one countries. With the exception of Africa, which at that stage had not declared any laboratory-confirmed cases (almost certainly due to a lack of laboratory testing rather than the absence of the virus), every WHO region had seen cases. The H1N1 virus was certainly global in its spread, of that there was no doubt. A large number of people had been affected. The dictionary definition of 'pandemic' seemed to have been met. Yet Margaret Chan, the WHO's Director-General, decided on that day not to declare a pandemic, apparently as a result of concerns about the panic that may have resulted (Gilman 2010). A month later, on 11 June 2009, and under significant pressure as a result of public concern, the WHO did declare a pandemic on the grounds that 'the scientific criteria for an influenza pandemic have been met' (Chan 2009).

Once it had declared a pandemic, the WHO came in for severe criticism. Questions were raised around the impartiality of its decision-making and whether or not severity ought to be part of the criteria for a pandemic declaration, given that this flu strain was now being recognized as relatively mild (Doshi 2011). The Parliamentary Assembly of the Council of Europe (2010) heavily criticized the organization for causing 'unjustified scares and fears about health risks', and raised the possibility that the pharmaceutical industry may have had an influence on 'some of the major decisions relating to the pandemic.' The WHO responded robustly, defending the impartiality of its expert advice and stating that 'WHO has not required a set level of severity as part of its criteria for declaring a pandemic. Experience shows that all pandemics cause excess deaths, that severity can change over time, and that severity can vary according to location and population' (WHO 2010). Nevertheless, whilst the WHO may have been technically correct in pointing out (as per the definitions above) that a pandemic is defined by spread not severity, it did a poor job of communicating this nuance to the general public and the media, leading to confusion and fear (Fineberg 2014: 1339).

This spat, which rumbled on for several months, revealed three important things for the discussion in this chapter. First, it highlighted the fact that the language that is used about outbreaks matters, and that the language used around infectious disease quickly becomes highly political. The term 'pandemic' is one example of this; 'health security' is another. Second, it showed that the WHO's pronouncements can have real implications for national and international security practices. The pandemic declaration triggered a range of actions at global, regional and national levels in line with the (then) guidance that 'For Phases 5–6 (pandemic), actions shift from preparedness to response at a global level. The goal of recommended actions during these phases is to reduce the impact of the pandemic on society' (WHO 2009: 41). Third, and finally, the controversy had implications for the way the WHO dealt with subsequent outbreaks. Having faced criticism for supposedly fear-mongering over swine flu, the organization later came under attack for being too slow to declare Ebola in West Africa an emergency. Some claimed the two were directly linked, arguing that 'the WHO may have hesitated to flag up the Ebola outbreak after it was accused of overhyping the 2009 H1N1 swine flu epidemic' (Flynn and Nebehay 2014).

Looking back on the 2009 H1N1 pandemic with the benefit of hindsight, it is easy to come to the conclusion that it was indeed the subject of excessive hype. This was not the next 'big one'. (At the time of writing this book, we are still awaiting the next 'big one' that, virologists warn us, will eventually emerge; Harmon 2011.) The fact that the terrifying mortality forecasts of some experts did not come to pass seems to legitimate a view that swine flu was never really a threat. Such feelings are a major contributor to what Price-Smith and Porreca (2016) have called the 'fear/apathy cycle'. But to dismiss the significance of the pandemic in this way misses three important points: that knowledge of the virus's virulence was developing as it spread across the world; that many people *did* die as a result of contracting the disease (as they do each year of seasonal flu); and that even if the consequences of the pandemic were less devastating than many feared, it nevertheless played into – and reinvigorated – longstanding narratives about the security threat posed by infectious diseases in a globalized world.

Global and National Health Security

In April 2001, the World Health Organization's Secretariat delivered a report to the World Health Assembly (the forum in which the Organization's 194 member states meet) entitled 'Global health security – epidemic alert and response' (WHO 2001). In that report, the authors neatly encapsulated the central set of claims at the heart of what has since become the well-established concept of 'global health security'. They said that

> The globalization of infectious diseases is not a new phenomenon. However, increased population movements, whether through tourism or migration or as a result of disasters; growth in international trade in food and biological products; social and environmental changes linked with urbanization, deforestation and alterations in climate; and changes in methods of food processing, distribution and consumer habits have reaffirmed that infectious disease events in one country are potentially a concern for the entire world. (WHO 2001: 1)

The key phrase here is the last one – that 'infectious disease events in one country are potentially a concern for the entire world.' In this single sentence the relationship between national and global health security is explicitly constructed. According to this view, it is impossible for states to insulate themselves from the threat of pathogens crossing borders (an idea to which we return in chapter 5). Diseases threaten national security, and in turn threaten global health security. The reverse is also true: national security depends on achieving global health security. According to this logic, far from being a zero-sum game between competing nations, security from disease requires global cooperation. The WHO, in the Secretariat's analysis, offered the best hope of delivering that cooperation, specifically through revising, strengthening and implementing a new set of International Health Regulations, the framework that since 1951 had set the template for international disease surveillance and response. More honoured in the breach than in the observance, those regulations were portrayed in the report as unfit for providing the collective security from disease that was now required. Urgent change was needed.

In 2001, these arguments found a propitious soil.[2] First, within public health communities (including the WHO) a rhetorical and conceptual shift had been under way for a few years from 'international health' to 'global health'. This, according to Brown, Cueto and Fee (2006) represented a move towards 'a consideration of the health needs of the people of the whole planet above the concerns of particular nations.' This was the emergence (at least rhetorically) of a very different way of understanding collective interests around the control of infectious diseases.

Second, and more directly, in the United States in particular, policy momentum around the security threat posed by infectious diseases had already been building from the late 1980s and through the 1990s. Joshua Lederberg, a molecular biologist, and Stephen Morse, a virologist, were two of the most prominent scientists calling for greater attention to be paid by the US government to the threat of what came to be known as 'Emerging Infectious Diseases' (EIDs). Both men were involved in a high-profile conference on 'Emerging Viruses' held in Washington DC in 1989, and both contributed to *Emerging Infections: Microbial Threats to the US*, a highly influential report published by the US Institutes of Medicine in 1992 (Lederberg and Oaks 1992). As Lorna Weir and Eric Mykhalovskiy (2010: 39) have argued, the 'invention' of the Emerging Infectious Diseases concept was a hugely significant step, capturing the attention of key US policy audiences (including security policymakers) and sensitizing them to the nature and scale of the threat.

This eventually resulted in President Bill Clinton issuing a Presidential Decision Directive (PDD) in June 1996 in which he stated that

> I have determined that the national and international system of infectious disease surveillance, prevention, and response is inadequate to protect the health of United States citizens from emerging infectious diseases ... I am calling for a series of actions to improve our surveillance, prevention, and response capability. (White House 1996: 2–3)

Soon afterwards, the US National Intelligence Council produced a National Intelligence Estimate on *The Global Infectious Disease Threat and Its Implications for the United States* (NIC 2000 [the report was written earlier, but only declassified in 2000]) that prominently featured exactly the types of arguments that Lederberg, Morse and others had been making in the preceding years. The National Intelligence Estimate naturally focused its attention on US national security, identifying the US as being a country particularly at risk because it is a 'major hub of global travel, immigration, and commerce with wide-ranging interests and large civilian and military presence overseas' (NIC 2000: 10). But the report also placed a heavy emphasis on the need for international cooperation in order to achieve security against disease threats, although it remained cautious about the likelihood of rapid improvements, noting that 'progress is likely to be slow, and development of an integrated global surveillance and response system probably is at least a decade or more away' (NIC 2000: 32).

Nevertheless, it is fair to say that by the late 1990s there was a strong and established narrative within the US national security community that, when it came to infectious disease threats, national and global security were intimately linked. The WHO Secretariat's 2001 report reflected and reaffirmed this narrative. The resolution adopted by the WHA in response (WHA 2001) asked the Secretariat to carry out further work on revising the IHR and called on member states to increase their efforts, both domestically and internationally, to improve surveillance, containment and response capacities.

A series of disease outbreaks over the next few years further reinforced the global health security narrative's claim that national and global health security are inextricably linked. The SARS outbreak of 2003 provided the most immediate and dramatic example of the ways in which EIDs could pose a threat not only to national security, but also to global security (Davies, Kamradt-Scott and Rushton 2015; Fidler 2003a). SARS was a previously unknown disease that, at some point in late 2002, somewhere in southern China, jumped the species barrier to infect humans. It came to worldwide attention in early 2003 when the virus arrived in Hong Kong, brought into the territory by a doctor visiting from mainland China. From Hong Kong, SARS rapidly spread around the world. By the time the outbreak was declared over in July 2003, 8,096 people in twenty-nine countries and territories had been infected. A total of 774 of them had died (WHO 2003). As well as the loss of life, SARS also provided a clear illustration of the economic impacts of outbreak emergencies in a globalized economy. As one example of its effects, Watson (2006: 201) reported that 'at the height of the SARS scare, the occupancy rate of Hong Kong's major hotels fell to 5 per cent, and it was rumoured that, on some nights in April 2003, two of the territory's grandest hotels did not have a single guest'. Although post-SARS analyses (e.g. Keogh-Brown and Smith 2008) suggested that the actual economic losses attributable to SARS had been much lower than some of the direst predictions at the time had forecast, they were nevertheless significant – a further motivation for governments around the world to take the EID threat more seriously.

The spread of H5N1 avian influenza (commonly known as 'bird flu') from 2004 and the H1N1 influenza pandemic of 2009–10 were again used to show the importance of global health security. These two strains of flu originated in different regions (the former in East Asia; the latter in North America) but quickly confirmed the well-worn truism that pathogens know no borders. Both illustrated exactly what Lederberg, Morse and their colleagues had argued many years before: that there was increased vulnerability to infectious diseases 'in a world represented as increasingly interconnected economically, socially, and microbiologically' (Weir and Mykhalovskiy 2010: 34). These diseases were seen as both a global threat and a threat to individual nations – a line that continued to be pushed strongly by the World Health Organization (WHO 2007) in its calls for strengthening the international disease surveillance and containment systems designed to ensure global health security.

Border Controls and Global Health Security

The narrative of global health security has a compelling logic: the security of any one state depends on global cooperation. It also leads to a clear set of policy prescriptions: we need to improve national and international capacities to perform key tasks in disease prevention, surveillance, containment and response. Failure to fulfil these functions anywhere in the world can endanger other countries – even ones that are geographically distant from the original source of an outbreak. This was one of the lessons most commonly pointed to during and after the 2014–16 West African Ebola outbreak. The weakness of health systems in

Guinea, Liberia and Sierra Leone led to what should have been at worst a localized epidemic becoming a regional problem, with, some argued, the potential to transform into a global pandemic. The policy recommendations identified by global health leaders and scholars in the aftermath of Ebola reinforced the global health security narrative. It is, it was argued, in the interests of the entire international community to give far more assistance to poorer countries in preparing for and responding to future such disease events (e.g. Gates 2015; Gostin et al. 2016; Moon et al. 2015). National health security rests upon global health security, which rests upon the ability of all countries – even the very poorest – to firstly detect and then respond quickly and effectively to outbreaks occurring on their territories.

The ability of countries to detect and contain outbreaks is not, however, the only obstacle to global health security. The unwillingness of governments to admit the existence of a domestic outbreak can also create risks. Sometimes they may be reluctant to do so for political reasons. Sometimes it may be out of fear of the economic consequences if other countries respond with travel and trade restrictions that prevent, for example, tourists entering or goods leaving. Advocates for international cooperation to achieve global health security have an answer to this. First, all countries need to be able to detect outbreaks quickly and reliably. Second, they need to be confident that when they disclose information about an outbreak occurring, they will receive support, not punishment, from other governments. Openness about outbreaks is in the interests of global health security. In the long term, openness depends on trust, which in turn depends on unaffected countries acting proportionately and responsibly to emerging outbreak emergencies to avoid disincentivizing future openness.

In this section, I argue that this clear and compelling logic comes under strain in the emergency politics that characterizes times of crisis. China's actions during the early stages of the SARS outbreak of 2003 are by far the most frequently discussed example of the failure of a government to get on board with the global health security idea, creating risks for other countries as a consequence. After initially attempting to cover up the emerging epidemic of this new and untreatable virus, China was later forced to concede that its actions had endangered the global community and to accept that in future it would have to approach such events in a more open and cooperative manner (Chan, Chen and Xu 2010). David Fidler argued in 2003 that China's actions over SARS 'proved a miscalculation of historic proportions. The miscalculation involves not only the damage China suffered but also China's failure to grasp the post-Westphalian context of infectious disease governance. The unfolding saga of the SARS outbreak in China tells the story of the humbling of the sovereignty of a rising great power' (Fidler 2003b: 492).

In some ways, however, SARS was a case where the lines of 'right' and 'wrong' were relatively easily drawn. China's early inaction on the public health front, and its egregious lack of transparency in communicating the risk both domestically and internationally, put in danger both its own citizens and the citizens of other countries in the region – and far beyond. Those failures led directly to the virus spreading beyond China's borders, and ultimately going on to infect over 8,000 people in almost forty countries. We might speculate, and many have, on the reasons for China's initial approach. The government's concerns probably included its desire to maintain domestic order and its international reputation, as well as its lack of ability to coordinate an effective response between the various ministries and agencies involved at different levels of government. When set against the consequences for global health security, this appears to be a simple morality tale. It is frequently represented as such in the global health security literature. Yet it is important not to let the benefit of hindsight, or our willingness to overlook the political contexts in which decision-makers operate, obscure our understanding of what can be very difficult policy choices in the context of an emerging crisis.

Place yourself in the shoes of a mid-ranking official in China's Ministry of Health in late 2002. There were reports of a mysterious pneumonia-like illness in Guangdong Province. Such information was seen by your political superiors as highly politically sensitive – and also as posing a threat to China's international trade if other countries were to respond by imposing import restrictions in an attempt to prevent the disease crossing into their territories. There was, under the 1969 IHR in force at that time, no formal requirement for China to report the outbreak to the WHO or anyone else. Your political career could be severely damaged if you used your own initiative to draw international attention to what was going on. Looking at this from the outside, you still might find that your sympathy for the mid-ranking Chinese health official is limited. A cog in an authoritarian machine, that official does what is best for their own career and what is most likely to please their political superiors, with potentially devastating consequences for global health.

But what if we place ourselves in a different set of shoes: those of a government minister in Côte d'Ivoire in August 2014, at the height of the West African Ebola outbreak? Since SARS, the new 2005 IHR had come into force. At the heart of these new rules was a reciprocal agreement: that countries would openly and quickly report to the WHO any outbreak on their territory that threatened to have international repercussions, and in return other countries promised that they would not impose unnecessarily harmful trade and travel restrictions on the reporting country. In August 2014, the WHO was recommending that neighbouring countries should not close their borders with Guinea, Liberia or Sierra Leone. But, at that time, the number of Ebola cases in Nimba county, Liberia (which borders Côte d'Ivoire) was increasing rapidly. The Ivorian government did close its borders in response, in an effort to prevent the virus – or, more accurately, individuals carrying the virus – from entering the country. Was this decision right or wrong? Speaking after the border was finally reopened two years later, government spokesman Bruno Kone was utterly unapologetic: 'We had to take these measures to protect our country. And the fact we didn't have a single case must be considered a real success' (Reuters 2016). As a national security measure, this approach was perhaps understandable, and appeared to be effective. At least in this case, it seemed, pathogens *did* recognize national borders. An outbreak of Ebola virus disease in Côte d'Ivoire would have been very bad news indeed, with a health system scarcely any better prepared to deal with the consequences than those in Guinea, Liberia and Sierra Leone. We might well understand, particularly in a situation where there is deep public anxiety about a deadly outbreak raging out of control across the border, why a government might decide that closing the border is the best course of action, even if it is contrary to the IHR's 'rules of the game'.

Senegal, which closed its border with Guinea in August 2014, justified doing so in ways that were, at least rhetorically, less narrowly concerned with the safety of its domestic population, although that was clearly an important factor. In an interview with the BBC, the Minister of Health and Social Action, Dr Awa Marie Colle Seck, argued that the border closure was a legitimate measure for two reasons. First, she argued that the WHO was still 'learning, like everyone', casting doubt on the robustness of the scientific evidence underpinning the WHO's recommendation not to close borders. Second, she argued that 'the countries surrounding those affected were a "sentinel for the world" and had a duty to stop the virus spreading further' (BBC News 2014). Here, then, we get a justification much more closely linked to ideas of global solidarity rather than national self-protection, problematizing dominant ideas about what is best for global health security and instead constructing a commonality of interest between national and global health security in a different way to the IHR, which prioritizes the longer-term functioning of international cooperation through maintaining openness, so far as possible, during times of crisis.

What if we were to take the example of Australia? Unlike Senegal and Côte d'Ivoire, Australia has no land border with any of the countries affected by Ebola. Perth, the closest major Australian city to West Africa, is well over 13,000 miles away from Monrovia, Freetown or Conakry. There are no direct flights to Australia from the region. Yet, in October 2014, Australia became the first high-income country to put in place travel restrictions against the three countries at the centre of the outbreak. Although the Australian authorities denied that the restrictions amounted to a travel ban, the Department of Immigration announced that it was suspending the issuing of visas for citizens of Ebola-affected countries, a suspension that was later extended to all foreign citizens who had visited an affected country. These measures were again in clear defiance of the WHO's recommended response (WHO 2014a). On 27 October 2014, Australia's Minister for Immigration and Border Protection Scott Morrison was asked in the House of Representatives by Nickolas Varvaris MP, 'Will the minister update the House on measures the government is taking to ensure the safety of all Australians given the outbreak of Ebola in West Africa?' Morrison's response, in which he justified the visa suspension, included the justification that 'The government systems and processes are working to protect Australians, and that is our focus in addressing this issue' (House Hansard 2014). In both the question and the answer the presumption that the safety of Australians was imperilled, and that immigration restrictions were necessary as a result, came through loud and clear.[3] This was reiterated by Morrison's later statement in the House, in which he said that 'These arrangements may inconvenience some travellers; however, the safety of the Australian community is paramount, and it is critical that Australia is not exposed to this disease. The government remains committed to protecting Australians and ensuring our border measures remain strong.'

Although geography makes this a very different case to Côte d'Ivoire or Senegal, we again might take the view that

Australia's decision to introduce travel restrictions was, from the point of view of the security of Australian citizens, an understandable course of action. Proponents of global health security like the WHO Secretariat argued that the closing of borders in the name of national security risked undermining the international cooperation that is essential to delivering global health security. Australia, which had little at stake in terms of trade with the region, and which was not going to receive any meaningful sanction for breaching the rules given the lack of enforcement powers at the WHO's disposal, decided on a 'safety-first' approach that also provided a measure of reassurance to a concerned public. But we can clearly see that short-term national security concerns led Australia to take actions that directly contradicted dominant ideas about what is required to realize global health security.

Reena Pattani (2015: 167) has argued that such conflicts between global and national security may be inevitable once security is invoked, that 'the very concept of global health *security* builds a "threat protection mentality" that risks emphasizing national sovereignty over global solidarity.' It is clear from the responses of Côte d'Ivoire, Australia and Senegal that the global and national visions of health security are currently in tension with one another. Even if we disagree with the approach taken by those governments during Ebola, we might nevertheless be able to understand the motivation for them. From the point of view of the global health security regime, however, all three countries (and many others) took exactly the wrong course of action. Notwithstanding Senegal's attempt to argue that containment within the region (via border controls) served the broader aim of global health security, the vast majority of advocates of global health security argued that such measures undermined global cooperation, hampered the emergency response effort, created new problems for the affected countries (e.g. around food importation), and were in any case likely to be ineffective. Prioritizing national over global security, they argued, actually increased the danger, both directly and indirectly. It also presented a long-term risk by undermining the relationships of mutual trust that are essential to the proper functioning of the IHR. If countries could not be relied upon to act proportionately and according to the rules, it was likely that others would attempt to keep outbreaks secret in future – as China did with SARS.

The Committee set up by the WHO to examine the operation of the IHR during the Ebola outbreak stressed the importance of the perceived fairness of the IHR framework, arguing that 'the IHR must be, and be seen to be, equitable across countries and ... all countries must be equally committed to full compliance, including not implementing measures beyond those recommended by WHO that are detrimental to countries reporting public health events' (Review Committee on the Role of the International Health Regulations (2005) in the Ebola Outbreak and Response 2016: 10). In order to achieve this, the committee encouraged the WHO to take stronger action in future cases where countries imposed 'additional measures' above and beyond those recommended by the WHO. In the Ebola case, although the WHO had requested an explanation from those countries that had gone beyond the recommendations (including imposing travel and trade restrictions), the majority of those countries failed to provide any such explanation, and suffered no consequences as a result. The IHR Review Committee encouraged the WHO to consider being more proactive in future, publicly naming and shaming states that fail to comply (Review Committee on the Role of the International Health Regulations (2005) in the Ebola Outbreak and Response 2016: 35–7).

Aside from being a threat to the proper functioning of the IHR, high-profile public health experts and international organizations also lined up to explain to governments why border closures were ineffective, and could even be counterproductive. Anthony Fauci, head of the US Centers for Disease Control and Prevention (CDC), explained that 'you could paradoxically make things much worse in the sense that you can't get supplies in, you can't get help in, you can't get the kinds of things in there that we need to contain the epidemic' (Fauci, quoted in Miller 2014). The UN Security Council, which passed a resolution on the Ebola outbreak in September 2014 (in which it determined – for the first time ever in relation to a disease emergency – that Ebola represented a 'threat to international peace and security'), was similarly concerned about the impact of travel and trade restrictions. Although it did highlight the importance of governments abiding by their IHR commitments (United Nations Security Council 2014: 2), the Security Council devoted a number of paragraphs to the practical as well as IHR-related implications of excessive travel and trade restrictions:

> 3. *Expresses concern* about the detrimental effect of the isolation of the affected countries as a result of trade and travel restrictions imposed on and to the affected countries;
>
> 4. *Calls on* Member States, including of the region, to lift general travel and border restrictions, imposed as a result of the Ebola outbreak, and that contribute to the further isolation of the affected countries and undermine their efforts to respond to the Ebola outbreak and *also calls on* airlines and shipping companies to maintain trade and transport links with the affected countries and the wider region;
>
> 5. *Calls on* Member States, especially of the region, to facilitate the delivery of assistance, including qualified, specialized and trained personnel and supplies, in response to the Ebola outbreak to the affected countries and, in this regard, *expresses deep appreciation* to the government of Ghana for allowing the resumption of the air shuttle of UNMIL from Monrovia to Accra, which will transport international health workers and other responders to areas affected by the Ebola outbreak in Liberia. (United Nations Security Council 2014: 4; emphasis in original)[4]

The African Union similarly urged its member states to lift travel bans, and called on governments to abide by the recommendations of the WHO in deciding their domestic policy responses (African Union 2014).

There is evidence that the already difficult situation being faced by Sierra Leone, Guinea and Liberia was exacerbated by trade and travel restrictions. Food imports were a particular area of concern. In Liberia, it was reported that the price of cassava increased by 150% in early August 2014 as cross-border trade slowed to a trickle (Bajekal 2014). The World Food Programme's monitoring of the food security impacts of the outbreak also found increasing market prices for many staples in parts of the most-affected countries (World Food Programme 2014), and even where prices did not rise, the reduction in household income suffered by many families caused a decline in food security (Thomas et al. 2014). Whilst not all of these problems were the result of border restrictions, it is clear that they did have a detrimental impact. It is not only national and global considerations that are in tension: human security can suffer too.

It is one thing for governments to agree in the abstract about the desirability of global cooperation in times of crisis, to embrace the symbiotic relationship between global health security and national health security, and to pledge international solidarity. But when a possible future outbreak becomes a real present-day crisis, the political calculation can shift dramatically – especially when the disease is understood in national security terms. Media pressure, public fear and a desire to err on the side of caution can all tilt the balance towards prioritizing domestic concerns about disease importation over the need to be a good international citizen.

History, the Future and the Global Health Security Narrative

In the previous section, I set out the clear logic of global health security, promoted by the WHO and others, in which global cooperation rather than national self-defence are the key to achieving sustainable collective security: that every state's national security ultimately rests upon the successful functioning of the global health security regime. In this section I argue that over time that logic is becoming increasingly powerful as the result of our experiences of disease in a massively globalized world, in the process conditioning how we think about future threats. Although, as we have seen, there are still incentives for policymakers to retreat to national self-interest in times of emergency, they do not always do so. The fact that most countries did comply with the IHR during the West African Ebola outbreak shows that security and trade interests were being balanced against one another, and suggests that the cooperative notion of global health security may not be an impossible dream. How and whether we can hope to move towards security with solidarity is discussed in the final section of the chapter.

The logic of global health security is to a great extent self-fulfilling. Once pandemics in general are identified as security threats, each new outbreak can potentially be used to prove the narrative is correct. Constructivist-derived analyses, such as that by Colin McInnes, have made the case that there is nothing inevitable or 'natural' about a particular disease outbreak coming to be recognized as a global security issue. Rather, that recognition emerges through a discursive process of social construction (McInnes 2016). The established ideas about global health security, however, may well increase the possibilities for such a construction becoming widely accepted, as new global disease crises fit with and become integrated into the narrative. It is striking that there is such a widely agreed roll-call, repeated in both the academic literature and the policy discourse, of globally significant twenty-first-century disease outbreaks, each of which, in its own way, has come to be seen as a landmark case that reinforces the global health security narrative. These run from SARS in 2003 through H5N1 and H1N1 in the first decade of the century, on to Ebola (2014–16). From each of these cases lessons have been identified (and in some cases *actually* learned). And each has reinforced the idea that an infectious disease outbreak emerging in any corner of the globe is a threat to all.

The global health security narrative has not only affected how we have responded to these epidemics and pandemics as they have occurred, it has also conditioned how we have come to think about the threat posed by potential future outbreaks. The past is seen as prologue, and each of these events has given rise to predictions of worse to come in the future. Influenza specialists have warned about the inevitability of a new and deadly pandemic strain emerging somewhere, sometime. Proponents of the One Health policy agenda have pointed to the increasing threat of new zoonotic diseases that could potentially kill far more than Ebola or SARS, a threat worsened as animals and humans increasingly compete for territory and come into contact as the result of deforestation and demographic changes. The rising threat of pathogens resistant to antibiotics and other antimicrobials has been identified as another future doomsday scenario, threatening the emergence of a 'post-antibiotic era' in which today's medicines become useless. Past experiences and future scenarios become fused together in the global health security narrative in ways that profoundly affect understandings of future insecurity.

Interestingly, even experiences of 'less severe' pandemics can bolster the narrative. The 2009–10 swine flu pandemic was widely interpreted as having been over-hyped, as high early estimates of mortality rates gave way to a view that this particular strain was in fact less deadly than seasonal flu. But whilst some spoke of such 'damp squibs' engendering 'pandemic fatigue', this does not seem to have transpired. Instead, swine flu became repackaged as 'the one we got away with' – a warning shot across the bows of an unprepared world that further highlighted the need to improve global systems and cooperation in preparation for the emergence of the *real* 'big one'.

There are, of course, reasons to be sceptical of the global health security narrative. As I argue in chapter 6, viewing global health history as periods of 'peacetime' punctuated by occasional emergencies is highly problematic, writing out the disease burdens that are everyday facts of life in the majority world in favour of a Global North-centric view in which infectious disease threats only impinge on our thinking in occasional short-term crises. Anticipating the likelihood of future outbreaks is notoriously hard, and whilst it may be true that some emergency response capabilities are generic, there is a danger that in 'fighting the last war' we remain ill-prepared for unknown pathogenic threats that may be just around the corner. Future scientific discoveries are also difficult to factor into our futurology. Many of the medical technologies of today could scarcely have been imagined even fifty years ago and future discoveries could mitigate or even eliminate some of the potential threats that preoccupy policymakers today. But at the same time (as I discuss in chapter 3) scientific advances can bring with them new forms of risk.

Faced with such enormous uncertainties, national public health and security policy communities have tended to fall back on traditional approaches to understanding risk in which they seek to assess, so far as can be known, the likelihood and potential impact of disease events on their own territories. Whilst they may well endorse the need for global cooperation in principle (and even engage in cooperative arrangements, such as strengthening global surveillance systems and committing to the IHR), during an emergency this cooperative spirit often comes under severe pressure. As we have seen above in examining Ebola-related border restrictions, during disease emergencies – especially proximate ones – many states turn their attention inwards and prioritize what they see as protecting themselves and their populations from external threats.

But not all states act in this way – at least not in all cases. During the West African Ebola outbreak, although some forty countries did exceed the WHO's recommended travel and trade measures, the majority did not. Those governments may have had a variety of reasons for playing by the rules. They may, for some reason, have felt less threatened than those that instituted border controls. They may have had greater confidence in the advice coming from the WHO. They may have decided that their interests lay in complying with their international commitments (in this case the IHR). For many, however, other interests seem to have outweighed the perceived threat of Ebola – not least interests in avoiding interrupting international travel and trade. These states did not pursue a 'maximum security at all costs' approach. Rather, they attempted to balance national security with the desire to keep the global economy moving.

Conclusion

In this final section of the chapter, I consider the possibilities of the global health security narrative being harnessed for greater solidarity. Will the demands of global and national health security always be inevitably in tension? Or are there political routes towards reconciling the two?

In a previous book (Davies, Kamradt-Scott and Rushton 2015), my co-authors and I made the case that the IHR 2005 had introduced some new international norms of global health security which, whilst certainly not universally adhered to, nevertheless opened up a possibility for gradually moving towards better global cooperation. The capacity-related constraints that we discussed in that book (in short, many governments simply don't have the health systems necessary to comply with the IHR, even if they wanted to) unfortunately remain. But has there been *any* progress on state willingness to comply? The West African Ebola case (which occurred after that book had been written, although before it appeared in print) seemed to suggest that any such progress has been limited. Many recommendations came out in the wake of that outbreak on the need to strengthen the IHR – and in particular to deal with the problem of non-compliance. The frustration that lay behind these recommendations was clear: how can governments be made to behave in a way that strengthens rather than undermines the cooperation needed to achieve global health security? How can we persuade governments to act according to longer-term collective interests rather than short-term individual ones? The answer to this question is about politics more than it is about international law (if it were even possible to separate those two). It is politics – international, but also domestic – that drives some governments towards deciding to impose border restrictions that run against what are proclaimed to be the interests of the global health security regime. But at the same time, it is only politics that can make the global health security regime work. Here I point to three areas of political challenge that must be grappled with if national and global health security are to be reconciled in the way that the WHO and other proponents of global health security hope.

The first is around government decisions to comply (or not) with their international obligations. Emergency politics of the type that we see during outbreaks is not the kind of politics that is likely to lead to the actions necessary to normalize compliance with the IHR. Instead, this is a job for politics in 'peacetime', between pandemics. It is for that reason that the 'lessons learned' processes that followed Ebola were important, and that implementation of their recommendations matters. The politics that is required here is one that appears to be apolitical, but in fact is not. It is the politics of bureaucratization and routinization that will lead to better compliance during outbreaks. If it becomes automatic for a state bureaucracy to report public health events of international concern to the WHO, and if it becomes almost automatic that the WHO's advice on the recommended responses carries significant weight in domestic decision-making, compliance will improve. This is not the same as saying that we will see universal compliance. But we will see more states complying more of the time. The low-level and unglamorous political work of institutionalizing cooperation is in many ways more important than the much higher-profile politics of denunciations, justifications and recriminations during an emergency.

Second, this also depends upon the wider politics of the WHO – an organization that is seemingly under constant attack from all angles. The WHO's daily activities through its relationships with national ministries of health and their IHR focal points – again low-profile and often unseen work – is an important part of institutionalization. But the WHO's actions during an emergency matter greatly as well. Its ability to influence governments rests on its reputation for providing good information and advice and its demonstrable independence from partial interests (whether that be influence by governments or industry). It is important not to underestimate the challenge of delivering on these things given the resource constraints the organization faces, and the complexity of its role. The WHO Secretariat must navigate these challenges both scientifically and politically, ensuring that the organization remains at the heart of the global health security regime in a world in which other actors, from global bodies like the UN Security Council to 'clubs of states' like the Global Health Security Agenda (GHSA), are expanding their remits.

Third, and vastly more complex to address, there is the public politics of pandemics. We know that fear and anxiety are common during pandemic scares (Aaltola 2012a; Ingram 2008), but we have far less of an understanding of how such fears can be alleviated where they are disproportionate to the risk. There has been a tendency to approach this as a question of risk communication: how can governments and bodies like the WHO better inform and reassure the public, how can the media be encouraged to report responsibly, and so on. But pandemic fear is far more deeply psychosocially embedded than that. It draws on cultural representations of disease, from Hollywood disaster movies to histories of the plague, and to even wider understandings of the world as zones of safety or danger. Crucially, it also relates to our fear of the diseased other, our horror of the carrier of disease and the belief that they represent a threat to us and our communities. All of this complex social politics has been prominently seen in relation to the virus to which we now turn: the Human Immunodeficiency Virus, which causes Acquired Immunodeficiency Syndrome (AIDS). In the AIDS case, some (although still far from sufficient) progress has been made in reducing disproportionate fears. It may provide lessons that can be applied elsewhere.

In some respects, as we will see in the next chapter, AIDS is unlike the rapidly spreading pandemics on which this chapter has focused. That difference is partly epidemiological, but it is also about the different ways in which we conceptualize diseases as security threats. In this chapter, the 'enemy' has been pathogens and their ability to spread (via human hosts) across borders, threatening to 'invade' new territories. In the AIDS case, we will see disease constructed as a security problem in a very different way, with different consequences for policy responses. The challenges in this chapter have been about balancing short-term perceptions of national interests with longer-term collective interests, and about balancing security with the continued functioning (so far as possible) of the global economy. In chapter 2, we will see that over time the most common policy solutions have shifted away from keeping the HIV virus out (given that the virus is already present in every country in the world) to attempting to change individual behaviours, in an effort to reduce the spread of the disease and limit its social, political and economic impacts.

− 2 −

AIDS: A Positive Case of Securitization?

In October 2016, a letter published in *Nature* (Worobey et al. 2016) finally cleared Gaétan Dugas's name once and for all. For years, ever since Randy Shilts's seminal book *And The Band Played On* (Shilts 1987), Dugas, a Canadian flight attendant, had widely been identified as the 'patient zero' of the North American HIV epidemic. Shilts's depiction of Dugas's behaviour on his annual week of San Francisco partying every June in the late 1970s was lurid, to say the least.

> Here [in San Francisco], Gaetan could satisfy his voracious sexual appetite with the beautiful California men he liked so much. He returned from every stroll down Castro Street with a pocketful of matchbook covers and napkins that were crowded with addresses and phone numbers. He recorded names of his most passionate admirers in his fabric-covered address book. But lovers were like suntans to him: They would be so wonderful, so sexy for a few days, and then fade. At times, Gaetan would study his address book with genuine curiosity, trying to recall who this or that person was. (Shilts 1987: 22)

With the 20/20 hindsight of 1987, when the HIV crisis was capturing headlines in the US and many other countries around the world, such sexual behaviour seemed reckless to the point of criminality. But whether Shilts's depiction of Gaetan's behaviour was fair or not, doubts about the identification of him as 'patient zero' gradually began to surface. In 2012, Shilts's editor

> admitted the book needed a literary device and [that he] had encouraged Shilts to create the epidemic's first 'AIDS monster'. The athletic sex life of Gaétan Dugas fit the bill nicely, and served as a symbol, deliberately or not, for everything people feared about gay sexuality. (King 2014a)

Worobey et al.'s 2016 analysis, derived from analysing the RNA of serum samples collected in the late 1970s, finally provided robust scientific evidence that Dugas had been wrongly accused of starting the American epidemic, showing that the virus was most likely introduced into the United States from an epidemic that was already under way in the Caribbean, first appearing in New York City in 1970 – long before Dugas came on the scene. Precisely how he came to be labelled patient zero in the first place is a difficult story to reconstruct. One explanation is the misreading of an epidemiological chart in which Dugas was labelled with an O (denoting 'Outside California') which was mistaken for a zero (Cohen 2016).

Gaétan Dugas himself died in 1984 and did not live to see the publication of Shilts's book, nor the docudrama of the same name in which his sexual behaviour was given a prominent role (Spottiswoode 1993). Although it is clearly unfortunate that Dugas was wronged in this way, it might be reasonable to ask whether, in the history of a disease that has taken many millions of lives and destroyed countless families and communities, it really matters. In this chapter I want to show that it does, because this case goes to the heart of understanding the trade-offs that we are faced with when weighing the pros and cons of viewing HIV and AIDS as a security threat. On the one hand, there are strong arguments to support the view that the framing of AIDS in security terms was an important factor in galvanizing national and international efforts to tackle the disease. But on the other, securitization is a strategy that can bring real human costs. The stigmatization of Dugas – in Mark S. King's words, *And The Band Played On* 'painted people with HIV as suicide bombers' (King 2014b) – represents the stigmatization suffered by countless other people living with HIV and AIDS (PLWHA) over the years since the Human Immunodeficiency Virus was first identified, people who have sometimes come to be seen as threatening to public health – and even entire nation states.

In International Relations, a good deal has been written on how HIV and AIDS came to be understood as a national and international security threat – a story that I trace in the first part of this chapter. Here we are confronted with a clear policy dilemma, where it is necessary to examine the pros and cons of a securitization strategy. But the AIDS case also offers an important vantage point for considering some more subtle security dynamics, moving our focus beyond the 'high politics' of national and international security considerations that were considered in the previous chapter, and towards how ideas of threat, danger and risk play out at a more human level. The modes of transmission of HIV brought into play a moralizing discourse that is less obviously apparent in many of the kinds of pandemic diseases discussed in the previous chapter. While few people would attach blame to someone who catches the flu virus, the same cannot be said of HIV. PLWHA – and Gaétan Dugas is a perfect example of this – have often been blamed for their own infection. What is more, they have often been seen as threatening. And, in a further extension of this threat/defence logic, whole communities have come to be understood as dangerous, and as posing risks to others. That such discourses are hugely problematic in ethical terms does not take away their power. But it does complicate the judgement of securitization as a political strategy. Could we have got political leaders to pay attention to AIDS without constructing it as a security threat? How can we take effective and well-founded public health measures to limit new infections without playing into these stigmatizing and discriminatory discourses? Can we ever avoid affected individuals and communities being seen by others as a threat?

In the final section of this chapter, I argue that AIDS is not only a case study of securitization, which is the way it has generally been treated in the International Relations literature. AIDS is also a case study of resistance, and in particular the resistance of PLWHA and their allies to the stigma and discrimination that are some of the biggest potential downsides of viewing AIDS as a security threat. Securitization has not excluded politics – far from it. It has run parallel to a vibrant, noisy and sometimes, for political leaders, awkward political movement that has made the case for human rights, social justice, inclusion and non-discrimination. Sometimes that movement has succeeded in winning the day.

The Construction of AIDS as a Security Threat

Whilst it may be an over-exaggeration to say that AIDS invented 'global health' – as has been claimed by Brandt (2013), for example – the UN Security Council's discussions of AIDS in 2000 certainly elevated its prominence, and subsequently that of global health more broadly, in academic International Relations (IR). As Colin McInnes and Kelley Lee, two of the pivotal figures in the development of health in IR, have noted, over the course of the early 2000s there was an explosion of interest in health, with it becoming well established by the end of the first decade of the new millennium as a recognized sub-field within the discipline (2012: 32–3). In many ways, however, as I argued in the Introduction to this book, IR as a discipline was late to the party. As we saw in chapter 1, scholars in Public Health had for many years been interested in the international politics of health, addressed first in the sub-discipline of 'international health', which later underwent a terminological shift to become 'global health'. In the policy world, too, the diplomatic and security dimensions of disease had been under discussion for a number of years. The lack of interest within academic IR through the twentieth century tells us more about the peculiarities of its disciplinary history than it does about the vibrancy of real-world global health politics.

But even if the year 2000 didn't herald the invention of a global politics of health, it certainly did mark a turning point in global efforts to tackle AIDS. By that point, the epidemics under way in many parts of the world were widely perceived to be of crisis proportions. UNAIDS' 2000 report on the AIDS epidemic estimated that 5.4 million people had been infected with HIV in 1999 alone, bringing the number of people living with HIV and AIDS worldwide to 34.3 million. Some 24.5 million of those were in sub-Saharan Africa, with South and Southeast Asia (at 5.6 million) the next hardest-hit region (UNAIDS 2000: 6). Peter Piot, the Executive Director of UNAIDS at the time, pointed out in his introduction to that year's report that the situation was far worse than most had predicted: estimates in 1991 had suggested that 9 million people in sub-Saharan Africa would be infected by the end of that decade. The reality was almost triple that number.

Even those much lower early predictions had raised concerns amongst security policy communities, especially in the US, about the medium- to long-term threat posed by AIDS. In 1987, only three years after HIV had been identified as the cause of AIDS, the CIA released a report on the implications of the virus for sub-Saharan Africa (CIA 1987). That report set out a range of concerns: that African leaders dissatisfied with Western assistance in tackling the crisis could turn to the Soviet Bloc for help; that African elites may be less likely to be sent abroad for education and could become 'excessively isolated and embittered and carry those negative views into future dealings with the world';

and that key economic sectors and agricultural production could be hit. The report also made a number of forecasts that later came to be central claims in the wider construction of AIDS as a security threat: that the effectiveness of militaries and security forces could be undermined, and that tensions between neighbouring countries could be inflamed.

In the following decade, AIDS had a prominent place in the US National Intelligence Estimate on *The Global Infectious Disease Threat and Its Implications for the United States*, discussed in the previous chapter. Again, the potentially destabilizing political and security impacts of HIV and AIDS were discussed; again, with a particular concern about the impacts on African armed forces, founded on the claim (that was later widely critiqued by, e.g., Barnett and Prins 2005) that infection rates in sub-Saharan militaries ranged from 10% to 60%, and were 'considerably higher than their civilian populations … [owing] to risky lifestyles and deployment away from home.'

By the late 1990s, then, the idea that AIDS could threaten military effectiveness as well as social, political and economic stability, most likely in sub-Saharan Africa, was well established as a concern amongst security policymakers in the US. The UN Security Council's discussions of the security implications of AIDS in January 2000 marked the successful internationalization of that concern (McInnes and Rushton 2010). That AIDS came to the Security Council was largely the result of concerted efforts by key individuals in the Clinton Administration, in partnership with UNAIDS, to highlight the international peace and security dimensions of the disease and to convince other governments of the urgent need for more decisive action. Richard Holbrooke, at the time the US Ambassador to the UN, was the driving force, getting the issue on the Security Council's agenda, convincing key colleagues in the Clinton Administration – including Vice-President Al Gore – to support holding a Security Council session, and persuading the Council's members to adopt Resolution 1308, which they did in July 2000. From the UNAIDS side, Peter Piot worked with Holbrooke to convince some reluctant members of the Council to put AIDS on the agenda. In that, Holbrooke and Piot faced significant resistance from Russia, China and France, all of whom felt that AIDS was beyond the Security Council's remit (Rushton 2010). The eventual persuasion of those states (albeit only to a certain extent – they succeeded in ensuring that Resolution 1308 focused on HIV in relation to UN peacekeepers, who are uncontroversially within the Council's remit) was a significant moment in the wider legitimation of the idea that AIDS could and should be understood as a disease with national and international security implications.

For both Holbrooke and Piot, whilst they did have genuine concerns about the security impacts of the disease, getting AIDS onto the Security Council's agenda was also part of a broader strategy to gain high-level political attention and commitment. Looking back in subsequent years, both saw this as having been a successful political move. Piot wrote that the Security Council's discussions were a 'tipping point' in the global response to AIDS:

> In the space of a year, it became an urgent, unavoidable subject for world leaders and organizations ... We succeeded in elevating AIDS to levels at which no health issue had ever been discussed before – to where the heavy lifting of international and national politics takes place. (Piot 2012: 273)

Holbrooke (2006), meanwhile, said that 'We were breaking the issue out of the field of health specialists and into the international consciousness as a security issue.' He recalled:

> Vice President Gore headed the U.S. delegation that day. The United States was in the presidency, and Al Gore did our nation proud by sitting in the seat as president of the Security Council and making a powerful speech, clearly and unambiguously identifying the AIDS problem as a security issue. And the world watched. It was one of the most

exciting days we had in the U.N., and I think history shows that it helped redefine the issue.

One of the reasons this moment attracted so much attention in academic IR was that scholars in that discipline, especially those interested in securitization processes, were also watching what was happening in the Security Council. This was a textbook example of securitization in which an issue previously not considered in security terms came to be constructed as a security threat, most directly to the more heavily-affected countries in the Global South, but by extension posing risks to regional and international security.

One of the main claims made for securitization as a political strategy is that it can call attention to an issue and encourage the expenditure of effort and resources to tackle it – just as Holbrooke and Piot argued had been done through their efforts in the Security Council. Yet the more critical scholarship that subsequently examined the securitization of AIDS worried about some of the downsides: that stigma and discrimination against people living with HIV and AIDS could be increased; that racialized ideas about 'dangerous' populations could be reinforced; and that effort could focus disproportionately on addressing the threat posed to militaries and security forces whilst neglecting less security-critical sections of the population (e.g. Elbe 2005).

The dilemma at the heart of this debate has been whether it was right to securitize AIDS. It is a question to which there is no simple answer. But it is an important one since similar strategies are still being applied to other health issues, perhaps most prominently in current policy discussions over the issue of antimicrobial resistance (see chapter 6).

Holbrooke and Piot had good reason to claim that this was a securitization success story. Governments in the Security Council publicly endorsed the idea that high levels of AIDS could come to pose a threat to national and regional security, with potential implications for states outside the region. After that, AIDS certainly had a far higher place on global policy agendas than it had previously enjoyed. This fed into a number of significant new developments. Perhaps the most notable of these was the creation of the Global Fund to Fight AIDS, TB and Malaria (the Global Fund) and the United States' President's Emergency Plan for AIDS Relief (PEPFAR). Between its founding in 2002 and the end of 2016, the Global Fund disbursed $32.6 billion to support HIV, TB and malaria programmes (the largest portion of this going to HIV) and claimed to have saved 22 million lives (Global Fund 2017). PEPFAR, meanwhile, rapidly grew to become the largest bilateral health assistance programme in history. By 2016, the US government had committed $72 billion to the programme, and claimed that it was supporting antiretroviral (ARV) treatment for 11.5 million people (PEPFAR 2016). Both PEPFAR and the Global Fund are shining examples of the new global commitment to both preventing and treating AIDS that came about around the turn of the millennium, hard on the heels of the Security Council's discussions of the subject in January and July 2000.

The strategic framing of AIDS as a security issue no doubt played a role in producing this new global commitment – and that commitment undoubtedly brought real improvements in the lives of PLWHA in terms of access to treatment, increased research and development efforts, and new initiatives in prevention and care. Yet it is difficult to isolate the influence of securitization from other things that were happening at the same time – including other ways in which HIV and AIDS were being framed. Certainly we may detect hints of security-driven thinking in some of what happened – including the very name of the President's *Emergency* Plan for AIDS Relief (Ingram 2010) – but elsewhere, other motivations for international action seem to have also been influential.

Perhaps the most important of these was the linking of AIDS to international development – an idea that became increasingly common in the late 1990s and was cemented in the MDGs, of which Goal 6 was 'Combat HIV/AIDS,

Malaria and other diseases'. The inclusion of AIDS in the MDGs bore witness to the political priority that the disease was at the time becoming, but it is less easily reducible to concerns over its security implications. Rather than being concerned with state stability or military effectiveness, in the AIDS and development discourse the concerns focused on a 'vicious circle' in which HIV and AIDS caused poverty, which in turn fuelled HIV infection; and the desirability of turning this into a 'virtuous circle' in which successfully tackling HIV epidemics in the most-affected countries would help reduce barriers to future economic development (Woodling, Williams and Rushton 2012). The Global Fund, indeed, was explicitly created as a means of funding the push to achieve MDG6 and some of its most influential proponents, not least the economist Jeffrey Sachs who headed the WHO's Commission on Macroeconomics and Health, were strong advocates of the need to invest in AIDS in order to promote economic development.

If security wasn't the only way in which AIDS was being framed, neither was the UN Security Council the only venue for global-level action. The General Assembly's Special Session on AIDS in 2001 (known as the UNGASS), indeed, was arguably an even more influential event than the Security Council's meetings on AIDS. At the UNGASS, UN member states adopted a 'Declaration of Commitment on HIV/AIDS'. Speaking at the time, then-Secretary-General Kofi Annan said that the UNGASS 'is historic for two reasons':

> First, the level of attendance shows that the world is at long last waking up to the gravity of the HIV/AIDS crisis. And second, the Declaration that will be adopted later this afternoon provides us with a clear strategy for tackling it. ... It is clear that all political leaders in important areas of both the developed and the developing countries are now taking this challenge very, very seriously. (Annan 2001)

This sentiment was echoed by Harri Holkeri, President of the General Assembly at the time, who described the

Declaration of Commitment as 'the first global "battle plan" against AIDS' (United Nations 2001). In subsequent years, the Declaration's status as an important touchstone has been maintained, and attempts have been made to measure progress against the commitments in it (Warner-Smith et al. 2009). But security reasoning was little in evidence in the UNGASS. Although mention was made in the Declaration of the potential for conflict to fuel HIV infection, and of the need to address the issue in both national militaries and UN peacekeeping forces, the framing of AIDS as an international development challenge was far more prominent.

These very different security and development framings of AIDS, occurring at the same time in different fora, greatly complicate any attempt to judge the extent to which securitization was crucial to attracting attention and resources, and by extension to answer the question of whether AIDS would have achieved a comparable level of global prioritization without securitization. We know that in certain international fora the security framing had traction. We know that some governments became concerned about security aspects of their domestic epidemics – see, for example, Roxanna Sjöstedt's work on the case of Russia (Sjöstedt 2008). We also know that there was a huge increase in international aid for AIDS. But we can't show the causality – it is impossible to separate out these different security and development motivations for putting effort and resources into tackling the pandemic. We certainly don't know what would have happened if the security discourse had not been present.

To further complicate the picture, the pandemic itself was getting markedly worse – and this was readily apparent to governments around the world. This naturally played into the securitization effort – indeed was the very basis of the construction of AIDS as an urgent crisis. But a growing momentum was already becoming clear before Holbrooke and Piot launched their Security Council strategy. Indeed, in the mid-1990s, there was plenty of evidence that the international community was beginning to wake up to the need to take action for health and humanitarian reasons.

The creation of UNAIDS, which began its work in 1996, was a clear indication of this. Intended to better harmonize the UN's efforts on AIDS (and also to rectify the perceived failures of the WHO's programme on HIV/AIDS, which was seen as insufficiently multisectoral), the new body broke new ground for the UN system – and at the same time became an influential new advocacy voice. As Elisabeth Pisani has described, the fledgling UNAIDS very much saw advocacy as an important part of its role (Pisani 2008: chapter 1) – a task that it approached in a variety of different ways through highlighting the humanitarian, development, human rights and (only later) international security implications of the disease.

AIDS drugs were also developing fast. Combination anti-retroviral therapies first became available in the mid-1990s, although initially at a price that led many to think that the large-scale roll-out of these new medicines in the world's poorest countries would be economically impossible – even with international assistance. By the early 2000s that picture had started to change. The Indian pharmaceutical producer Cipla introduced the first generic versions of combination ARVs in 2001, significantly reducing the price (from $10,000 per patient per year to, initially, $1,200 per year and later less than $100 a year), resetting debates over the feasibility of improving access in the developing world. Without this major change in the economics of treatment, it is almost impossible to imagine the Global Fund being created – still less the G8 making a commitment to ensuring ('as close as possible to') universal access to treatment, as they did at the Gleneagles Summit in 2005 (G8 2005) – even if there had been a perceived security threat. As discussed in the final section of this chapter, concerted efforts by AIDS advocates and affected communities around the same period, largely drawing on human rights rather than security claims, also played an important role in demanding lower prices for drugs, sensitizing governments to the need for greater international assistance, and improving access to prevention, treatment and care services around the world.

There are plenty of good reasons to be sceptical of the motives of governments of the Global North in their international aid efforts. But to argue that (Global North) governments *only* began to care about AIDS because they came to see the pandemic as a potential national and international security threat is something of a stretch. This was *one* of the reasons that *some* influential governments saw it as necessary to increase their efforts. And *some* of the new assistance was clearly oriented in a security direction. Most obviously this could be seen in programmes designed to assist African militaries to improve diagnosis, prevention and treatment within their ranks. Some have also argued that the initial targeting of PEPFAR funds to 'focus countries' – a list that did not map neatly onto the most-affected countries – could have been driven in part by security and geopolitical considerations (Emanuel 2012; Ingram 2011). But even without entirely dismissing the significance of securitization as an effective political strategy in the AIDS case, we should at least call into question the idea that AIDS was the archetypal 'successful securitization'. Having considered whether the upsides were as great as is often believed, this chapter now turns to look at the downsides of securitizing AIDS.

Risky People and Threatening Communities

Securitization theorists have generally been concerned about securitization as a political strategy, claiming, amongst other things, that security-driven responses to 'threats' such as infectious diseases have a disturbing tendency to lead to anti-democratic emergency responses in which the rights and liberties of individuals get trampled. These concerns were especially prominent in the AIDS case given the long history of stigma and discrimination faced by many of the communities that were most affected in the early years. The identification of new outbreaks of an as-yet unidentified disease in San Francisco and New York in the early 1980s quickly led to attention being focused on high infection rates in the gay community. As the sexually transmitted nature of the virus became clearer, attention turned to sexual behaviour amongst members of that community – as exemplified by Randy Shilts's description of Gaétan Dugas quoted at the beginning of this chapter. This new threat, and concerns about the danger of the infection spreading into heterosexual communities, added to the stigma and discrimination that gay communities already faced. The same is true of most of the other groups that also came to be seen as particularly at risk, not least intravenous drug users and sex workers.

What emerged in the 1980s, initially in the US but soon reflected elsewhere in various forms, was a discourse in which the '4Hs' – haemophiliacs, heroin addicts, homosexuals and Haitians (Gallo 2006) – came to be seen as posing a threat to wider society. Although at this stage these fears were more commonly expressed in moral and religious terms (as seen in the common phrase 'gay plague') rather than as national or international security threats, the kinds of threat/defence logics that are redolent of security thinking were well in evidence, as was the identification of supposedly 'dangerous' individuals and communities.

Where national security considerations came to be more explicitly apparent was once the US government began to see AIDS as, in part, an external threat – especially around the Haitians of the '4Hs'. The George H.W. Bush Administration's quarantining of Haitian refugees at Guantanamo Bay in the early 1990s (discussed at greater length in chapter 4) was a particularly egregious attempt to prevent the entry of HIV-infected refugees onto the US mainland (Farmer 2003: chapter 2; Johnson 1994). The same defensive logic was also evident in the entry restrictions imposed by the US and many other countries on PLWHA – restrictions that are still in place in a number of countries today.

There have, then, been security-driven efforts to prevent the importation of HIV – not too dissimilar to the border controls that we saw in chapter 1 – that have infringed on the rights and liberties of PLWHA. It is more difficult, however, to find cases where security-driven international assistance programmes for AIDS have directly caused human rights abuses. For sure, there have been many abuses of the rights of PLWHA, but for the most part these have not emerged as a result of national and international security considerations. Rather, they have ben rooted in other policy drivers (for example, the religious beliefs that lie behind the highly controversial 'global gag rule'), or from more deeply embedded forms of stigma and discrimination.

As the epidemic has become more well established, in some places even normalized, we have slowly seen a reduction in explicit discrimination and a rejection (at least rhetorically) of some of the threat/defence logics that characterized the AIDS policy discourse in many places in the 1980s. Although it is important not to underestimate the extent to which stigma and discrimination persist, securitization has actually coincided with a reduction in officially-sanctioned discriminatory practices in most parts of the world. To some extent, then, we have seen the opposite of what some feared. How can we explain this? Here I offer two complementary explanations, before going on in the final section of this chapter to examine a third.

First, unlike the rapidly-spreading diseases examined in chapter 1, even where HIV was seen as a threat to national and international security, the response required to counter that threat was one largely rooted in public health rather than in traditional security practices. With the exception of controls at the border (which, as we have already seen, some states did, and still do, deploy), the weight of scientific evidence quickly came to show that community-based interventions in prevention, treatment and care were the most effective way of getting to grips with HIV epidemics. What was needed was to change behaviours to reduce the spread of the virus (for example through advocating condom use and educating intravenous drug users on the risks of sharing needles), and to make sure that those already infected were receiving treatment, both improving their health and well-being and reducing the chances of them infecting others. By the mid-2000s, these approaches had begun to bear fruit: globally new infections reached their peak in 2005 and then began to decline, while the proportion of those eligible for treatment who actually received it grew rapidly as a result of international funding sources like the Global Fund and PEPFAR, as well as national investments. Stigma and discrimination were identified by public health experts as being major obstacles to the effectiveness of these responses. Stigma and discrimination led people to avoid being tested, increasing the risk to their own health and that of others, and made it challenging for people to adhere to treatment regimens and to access the other care they needed. Thus, reducing the risk that AIDS was believed to pose to political and economic stability in sub-Saharan Africa and other heavily affected regions meant taking long-term actions that were guided by public health evidence rather than the kinds of explicitly authoritarian top-down emergency responses that are often seen as the downsides of securitization.

Second, as already noted, securitization wasn't by any means the only game in town. In addition to international development thinking, particularly important in the AIDS case were human rights ideas, which came to be central to the AIDS response from a very early stage. Jonathan Mann, who first headed the WHO's Global Programme on AIDS, was a particularly influential voice for a rights-based approach, both on ethical grounds and because he saw such an approach as central to effective public health practice. As a result of the efforts of Mann and many others, human rights, and the inclusion of affected communities in decision-making (captured in the concept of 'GIPA' – the Greater Involvement of People with AIDS), became deeply embedded in AIDS policy at the global level – and to an extent was also reflected at the national level in many countries. In comparison with other diseases, AIDS policy was marked by a high level of vigilance around the protection of the rights of those affected by the disease, either directly or indirectly.

Activism and Resistance

Although the public health and human rights focus of high-level policy communities was a more notable feature of the AIDS response than we have seen around many other diseases, in this section I argue that the primary reason that some of the often identified downside risks of securitization in the post-2000 era have been reduced in the case of AIDS, particularly those that relate to rights-abusing authoritarian responses, has been because of the strong and vibrant history of AIDS activism. PLWHA, the most-affected communities, and their allies, have not just been acted upon: they have been actors, powerful and influential enough to have major impacts on policies, programmes and agendas. Studies of securitization tend to be top-down in orientation, focusing – as this chapter did in describing the securitization of AIDS – on elite-level speech acts and national and international decision-making processes. To approach the history of national and international action on AIDS solely in this way would completely fail to capture the essence of the story. There was, from the very early days, a vibrant movement rooted in grassroots activism, initially in the face of elite indifference – indeed outright hostility.

The history of organizing amongst gay communities, most famously in San Francisco and New York, in the early days of the AIDS crisis is well known, and has been the subject of countless books and films. Groups such as ACT UP became far more than just campaigning groups, over time also becoming important sources of education, solidarity and support (Gould 2009). But ACT UP and other groups like it certainly were powerful lobbying voices, targeting the US government, the National Institutes of Health, the pharmaceutical industry and others over their apparent lack of urgency in investing in the research and development needed to find ways of tackling the epidemic. These groups developed significant scientific expertise, allowing them to engage with policymakers and scientists as experts in their own right (France 2016), and they also played an important advocacy and 'watchdog' role, maintaining maximum vigilance for both implicit and explicit signs of discrimination, battling stigma, and making a case for rights-based responses to the epidemic. This early concern with stigma and discrimination came about partly because of the communities within which the disease was first recognized, communities that had faced long-standing discrimination. But it was also partly due to the reactions of the public, media and politicians to HIV specifically. Terms such as 'gay plague' were a common feature of the early public discourse on AIDS (e.g. Daily Telegraph 1983). Patrick Buchanan, the right-wing US commentator, famously wrote in 1983 that 'The sexual revolution has begun to devour its children. And among the revolutionary vanguard, the Gay Rights activists, the mortality rate is highest and climbing' (cited in Shilts 2007: 311). Although they were not so openly expressed, it seems certain that such views were also present within the Reagan Administration. Reagan himself didn't even use the word 'AIDS' in public until 1987, and, when asked what people should do about AIDS, he replied 'Just say no' (Gill 2006: 10).

Combatting stigma and discrimination was not only an ethical concern for early AIDS activists, but also a practical one. It quickly became apparent that the stigmatization of PLWHA made it far less likely that people would come forward for testing, and far less likely that adequate services would be provided to those found to be infected with the virus. Stigma also made it less likely that governments and the pharmaceutical industry would devote time and resources to developing new drugs to fight the disease. Rights-based activism and resistance to discrimination were central to creating the momentum that led to AIDS becoming a high-profile public and political issue – and long predated the widespread use of a national security frame of reference.

Just as it is important not to write out the influence of PLWHA and allied activists, so it is important not to make the story a US (or event Western)-centric one. Resistance in and from the Global South has also been central to the history of the global AIDS response, and has often led rather than followed elite-level policy action. Again, activists have forwarded discourses that are radically divergent from the idea that AIDS should be treated as a national security threat. These two discourses have generally followed separate but parallel tracks: an elite discourse focusing on security (and international development) reasons to be concerned with AIDS, and a grassroots one addressing the humanitarian, human rights and social justice aspects of the global response. The success of the latter can be seen clearly in two of the most significant achievements of the AIDS movement: establishing the principles of the universal access to antiretroviral medications (ARVs) and GIPA. In neither case has the reality quite lived up to the theory. But in both, advocates have succeeded in leading the way in global health through campaigns that have actively opposed the exclusionary and discriminatory practices that often characterized early responses to the disease (and which, in some parts of the world, are unfortunately still in evidence).

The battle for the recognition of the right of PLWHA to have access to antiretroviral medicines was hard fought, both in national contexts and at the international level. The work of the Treatment Action Campaign (TAC) in South Africa has been particularly widely covered, and was totemic for the wider global campaign to establish the right to access these life-changing medicines (Geffen 2010; Mbali 2013). The legal cases brought by the TAC challenged the Mbeki Administration's denialism, and eventually forced the South African government to accept its constitutional duty to provide treatment for its citizens. Although in practice access to treatment is still far from 'universal' in South Africa, the principle that it *ought to* be has itself had a dramatic impact, putting pressure on the government to fulfil its constitutional responsibilities.

Even South Africa, a relatively wealthy country by sub-Saharan African standards, faces major difficulties in delivering this scale of treatment to its people, notwithstanding the significant decreases that have been seen in the cost of providing ARVs to each individual. Poorer countries with similarly high prevalence rates face an even bigger challenge. For that reason, establishing the idea that there was a global responsibility, and not just a national one, for realizing the right of PLWHA to access treatment was crucial. As discussed above, the establishment of the Global Fund and PEPFAR brought about a major expansion in access, but the G8's 'Renewed Commitment to Africa' at the Gleneagles Summit in 2005 represented a particularly significant moment in the acceptance of a global responsibility to provide treatment, with the world's richest countries promising to pursue 'the aim of as close as possible to universal access to treatment for all those who need it by 2010' (G8 2005: para. 18(d)). Whilst the decision-makers at Gleneagles who agreed this statement were of course political elites, this commitment would have been unthinkable without the backdrop of global advocacy and activism, led by PLWHA and allies, churches and many other civil society organizations, and coming to a head (not only around AIDS, but also issues such as Third World Debt) with the Live 8 concerts and lively demonstrations that immediately preceded the Summit. A month earlier, writing in *The Guardian*, UK Chancellor of the Exchequer Gordon Brown said that 'Years from now, people will ask of AIDS and Africa: "How could the world have known and failed to act?"' (Brown 2005). In fact, people were already asking that, loudly and clearly. If they had not been, it is impossible to imagine that the political pressure would have been sufficient to motivate the massive increase in resources for HIV treatment (and also prevention and care) that were seen from 2000 onwards.

The same is true of GIPA. This is the principle that those affected by AIDS have the right to have a place within AIDS governance arrangements – often captured in the phrase 'nothing about us without us'. Simple in theory, this in fact required a massive shift in traditional ideas about appropriate governance structures at both the national and international levels. Multilateral bodies traditionally have governance arrangements in which only member states are represented, but the Global Fund has included representatives of affected communities on their board, and UNAIDS has five NGO representatives on its Programme Coordinating Board – the first time ever a United Nations programme had formal civil society representation on its governing board. These achievements were again thanks to the demands of advocates and PLWHA over many years. The principle of GIPA has now become so well established that it has come to be seen as crucial to the legitimacy of AIDS initiatives at all levels.

In both of these cases, we see that politics was *productive*, not simply an obstacle. Crucially, activists operating at all levels, from grassroots communities right up to global level summits, were involved in framing AIDS in ways that were about rights, justice and solidarity far more than they were about national and international security. True, the elite attention grabbed by the security arguments around AIDS may well have helped make the soil more fertile for such advocacy efforts, but at the same time activists were on the look-out for policies and practices that were stigmatizing, discriminatory, or which showed evidence of any of the other feared downsides of securitization.

Conclusion

AIDS seems to be a case where some of the cons of securitization have been guarded against relatively (although not entirely) successfully. This was a result of determined political action, and much credit must go to the activists around the world who were (and remain) ever watchful for policy responses that promote stigma and discrimination, or which position PLWHA as a threat to others.

But whilst securitization has not been as detrimental as some feared in terms of adding to stigma, discrimination and other abuses of rights, there have been other trade-offs that relate not to rights but rather to prioritization. AIDS has occupied such a prominent position on the global health and development agenda that some have worried about those things that seem to have been crowded out – an issue to which we will return in chapter 6. A very sensitive debate has emerged about whether too much money has been spent on AIDS in the period since 2000. Whilst few critics have been willing to put themselves in the invidious ethical position of arguing that less should be spent on AIDS, some have questioned whether the correct balance has been struck. Roger England was one of the most prominent such voices, arguing that some of the money being dedicated to AIDS could be better spent elsewhere (England 2007; see also Smith 2009). AIDS activists have, understandably, reacted furiously to such views, arguing that 'the solution is not to divide up the small funding pie, but to make the pie bigger' (Treatment Action Campaign 2009).

Nicoli Nattrass and Gregg Gonsalves (2009) also took up the case for AIDS spending, arguing that the critics underestimated the effects that the inflow of AIDS-focused resources had had on improving health and health systems more broadly in the Global South. The debate over whether AIDS has had a 'halo effect' on global health continues. Allan Brandt, a historian of science and medicine, has argued that AIDS represented a transformational moment in global health:

> The changes wrought by HIV have not only affected the course of the epidemic: they have had powerful effects on research and science, clinical practices, and broader policy. AIDS has reshaped conventional wisdoms in public health, research practice, cultural attitudes, and social behaviors. Most notably, the AIDS epidemic has provided the foundation for a revolution that upended traditional approaches to 'international health,' replacing them with innovative global approaches to disease. Indeed, the HIV epidemic

and the responses it generated have been crucial forces in 'inventing' the new 'global health.' (Brandt 2013)

Much of this seems to be borne out by the evidence of the last two decades. But whether, in economic terms, AIDS spending led to a concomitant increase in spending on other global health issues is more debatable. Shiffman et al.'s analysis suggests not, finding that funding for broader health system strengthening efforts stagnated through the 'boom years' of AIDS spending (Shiffman, Berlan and Hafner 2009).

As the Millennium Development Goals deadline of 2015 began to come closer, attention turned to agreeing a new set of goals to succeed the MDGs – which eventually went on to become the Sustainable Development Goals. During this negotiation process, the idea that AIDS had received disproportionate attention in the MDG era really began to bite. Advocates for other health challenges pushed the case for 'their' issue being included in the next set of global goals, and proponents of 'horizontal' health systems strengthening efforts (as opposed to 'vertical' efforts targeted at specific diseases like AIDS) also made their case vociferously. Many in the AIDS community worried about the impact of a possible deprioritization of AIDS on the sustainability of existing programmes, and also on the long-term efforts to eradicate the disease. Ultimately, it would be fair to say that AIDS does have a much lower profile in the SDGs as compared to the MDGs – although it isn't absent entirely. Whereas in the MDGs HIV, along with malaria and 'other diseases', had been the focus of Goal 6 – one of the three 'health MDGs' – in the SDGs the single overarching health goal (Goal 3: Good Health and Wellbeing) included 13 subsidiary targets, of which AIDS was included in one (3.3: By 2030, end the epidemics of AIDS, tuberculosis, malaria and neglected tropical diseases and combat hepatitis, water-borne diseases and other communicable diseases). AIDS still has a place in the SDGs as one of the priority global health challenges, but it is now more difficult to argue that it dominates the international agenda. In terms of funding, there are early signs of decline: the amount provided by donor governments for HIV and AIDS fell 7% between 2015 and 2016 (Avert 2017). This certainly provides some early evidence of the feelings of many that global political interest in AIDS as a global health policy priority is beginning to wane.

In this chapter, we have seen a different relationship between disease and security to that which we saw in chapter 1, and very different types of policy effort designed to mitigate the perceived threat. Unlike rapidly spreading pandemics, where the emphasis has been on rapid identification and containment, trying to keep the diseases out of so-far unaffected territories (at least, so far as possible in a globalized world), the perceived security dynamics in the case of AIDS (which is already present everywhere) have been around the impact of extremely high prevalence rates. And whilst it is true that border controls have (too often) been enacted by governments around HIV and AIDS, a consensus has emerged over time that effective policy responses are much longer term and are based on positive engagement with affected communities rather than trying to exclude them. Behaviour change to reduce transmission and the roll-out of treatment globally are the solutions to the AIDS crisis – whether one sees it as a security crisis, a development crisis, or a humanitarian crisis. As a result, the tensions between these different ways of approaching AIDS as a policy problem have not been as stark as was feared in earlier days. In the Conclusion to this book, I suggest that this may offer a model for a longer-term and less emergency-oriented approach to dealing with global health security threats.

The dream scenario for the AIDS community is that an effective vaccine, or a drug that offers a cure, will one day be developed, and the pandemic brought to an end. Research efforts in pursuit of those goals continue. The idea that scientific progress will ultimately enable us to triumph against AIDS and other diseases is a common one. But as well as offering solutions, science can also generate new policy dilemmas, and new forms of risk. In the next chapter, we will see yet another way in which disease-related issues have been framed in security terms – and once again a very different set of policy options available to governments seeking to mitigate the threat.

− 3 −

Science, Risk and Uncertainty

On the morning of 1 July 2014, on the campus of the National Institutes of Health in Bethesda, Maryland, a researcher from the Food and Drug Administration who was clearing out an old cold store room found twelve cardboard boxes that had lain undisturbed for decades.[5] In those boxes, amongst 327 vials containing biological samples of various infectious diseases, were six that contained variola, the virus that causes smallpox. That discovery led to a rapid biosecurity response and the building being put on lock-down. An investigation was opened into how the samples came to be there, and what lessons could be learned from the incident (Blue Ribbon Panel 2017).

The discovery of these six vials was important because smallpox has been eradicated in the wild – arguably one of the greatest human achievements of the twentieth century. As the World Health Assembly's 1980 Resolution officially declaring the end of smallpox put it, 'the world and all its peoples have won freedom from smallpox, which was a most devastating disease sweeping in epidemic form through many countries since earliest times, leaving death, blindness and disfigurement in its wake' (WHA 1980).

Following eradication, an agreement was reached that all remaining samples of the virus were to be transferred to two secure laboratories: the Soviet Union's State Research Center of Virology and Biotechnology (VECTOR) in Novosibirsk (in present-day Russia), and the Centers for Disease Control and Prevention (CDC) in Atlanta, Georgia. The six vials found in Bethesda had somehow slipped through the net, leading security officials to wonder how many other long-forgotten variola samples might be out there somewhere – and who might find them. The possible nightmare scenarios include two possibilities that run as themes through this chapter. First, that an accident or mistake at VECTOR or CDC, or at another location where samples have either accidentally or deliberately remained, could lead to the virus escaping, undoing the work of global eradication and taking away humanity's hard-won freedom from smallpox. Second, samples of the virus could fall into the hands of terrorists, a rogue state, or some other nefarious group or individual who might use, or threaten to use, smallpox as a biological weapon.

Given these twin risks, there have been regular debates over the last 30 years about whether the variola samples at VECTOR and CDC should just be destroyed, removing (or at least substantially reducing) the possibility of a future escape. The US and Russia have thus far resisted these calls for destruction, primarily on the basis that the samples still have value for scientific research – research that could be extremely important if smallpox or some other similar virus were somehow to return.

Meanwhile, advances in the life sciences might soon make this policy dilemma obsolete. Developments in the field of synthetic biology have put scientists on the brink of being able to artificially create the variola virus using DNA synthesis technology. It might even have happened by the time this book is published. Governments face some difficult policy problems in attempting to regulate this rapidly advancing area of science, where potential threats come not just from determined adversaries, but also from the activities of legitimate and well-intentioned scientists, or from 'amateur hobbyists' engaged in 'homebrew' biological experiments.

In this chapter I argue, in line with the overall thrust of the book, that the choices policymakers face in attempting to protect populations from such threats are inherently political, not merely technical. They are, at heart, about striking a careful balance: how much security do we want, and what are we prepared to forgo in order to achieve it?

In the case of deliberate biological attacks, governments come up against choices that require the balancing of security concerns on the one hand with the opportunity costs of investing in biodefence programmes of uncertain effectiveness on the other. Furthermore, such biodefence programmes can in themselves create new risks. In the case of dangers emerging from well-intentioned scientific work, where the threats may emanate from accidental releases, or misuse of scientific knowledge by others, rather than deliberate acts by the scientists involved, a different trade-off is in play: between creating an environment in which new scientific breakthroughs can be achieved and academic freedom can flourish, and exposing the public to an unacceptably high level of risk. Finally, where non-professional life-scientists are concerned, difficult questions about the appropriate level and manner of regulation, and how effective it can be, are raised. Having the potential to create enormously valuable breakthroughs for the future of humanity, and at the same time to create significant risks of deliberate or accidental pathogen release, the biosciences are therefore a thorny political and policy problem.

This chapter works through these three separate, but closely related, areas in turn, critically exploring contemporary attempts to strike a balance in each, discussing the trade-offs that are at stake, and arguing that in all cases good policymaking is hampered by the inability to quantify either the risks or the benefits. The likelihood of the worst-case scenarios coming to pass is impossible to judge with any degree of certainty, making it difficult to determine the value of investing in biodefence. Meanwhile, the possible future benefits of scientific research are inherently unknown. I conclude the chapter by discussing the importance of political debate in this field, and especially of life scientists themselves being active participants in that debate, to educate and help governments in navigating the complex regulatory challenges.

Biological Weapons, Bioterrorism and Biodefence

Works on biological warfare commonly start with a reflection on the long history of the phenomenon: on the use of diseased carcasses to poison enemy wells in antiquity; on the distribution of smallpox-ridden blankets to infect native American communities; and on towards the present day. Dramatic developments in the biological sciences in the late nineteenth and early twentieth centuries opened up the way for far more sophisticated methods of developing and delivering biological weapons than had ever been seen before. The discovery of germs and viruses, and the ability to isolate and culture them in the lab, made it feasible for militaries to seriously investigate their potential as weapons of war. Germany experimented with using anthrax and glanders during the First World War, although in a relatively small-scale way. A number of other countries developed national biological weapons programmes in the inter-war period (Frischknecht 2003). The Japanese use of biological weapons in the Second World War was the largest-scale deployment of this kind of weapon to date, including the use of cholera, typhus and plague (Harris 2002).

After the Second World War, and into the early years of the Cold War, research on both biological weapons and biodefence countermeasures intensified, particularly in the Soviet Union and the USA, but also elsewhere. President Richard Nixon's decision to unilaterally renounce the use of biological weapons and to sign the Biological and Toxin

Weapons Convention (BWC) in 1972, however, signalled a significant shift. Despite its limitations (most notably the absence of an effective verification mechanism), the Convention was seen as a major step towards a bioweapon-free world in that it prohibited not only the use of biological weapons but also the development, production and stockpiling of them – although it left the door open to states carrying out research using potential bioweapon agents for peaceful and defensive purposes.

Nevertheless, biological weapon research continued apace, with a huge secret programme continuing in the Soviet Union involving the weaponization of a wide range of pathogens and the stockpiling of large amounts of biowarfare material. Much of what is known about these programmes was only discovered after the collapse of the Soviet Union (e.g. Leitenberg and Zilinskas 2012). Whilst a similar quantity of information has not to date emerged in relation to American activities during this period, it seems highly likely that 'offensive' research in fact continued, to some extent at least. One of the issues that has plagued the BWC has been a lack of clarity over what constitutes 'offensive' as opposed to 'defensive' research and, as Christian Enemark (2017: 8–14) shows, the Soviet Union had strong suspicions that the US's ostensibly 'defensive' programme was in reality a cover for ongoing work on developing biological weapons in secret. Such suspicion is probably not surprising given that, as Enemark points out, even legitimately 'defensive' R&D requires the development of potentially offensive capabilities (such as dispersal systems and, as we will discuss later in the chapter, the weaponization of anthrax) in order to test new defensive technologies.

In the post-Cold War era, concerns shifted to 'rogue states' – including Iraq, Iran, North Korea, Libya, Syria and others – who have all been suspected at one time or another of having active biological weapons programmes. In general, however, the modern history of states using biological weapons during war is relatively limited, certainly in comparison to chemical weapons. There is probably no

single reason for this, but rather a range of factors including the difficulty of developing effective biological weapons,
the ready availability of other means of waging mass-casualty
warfare, a lack of belief in the strategic utility of biological
weapons, and, perhaps, the existence of a widely held
international norm (codified in the BWC) that the use of
such weapons is not legitimate.

Despite the attention it has received, there is a similarly
limited history of bioterrorism. It is, of course, dangerous
to tempt fate, but one of the most perplexing things about
bioterrorism is that we have not seen more of it. The technology to create and deliver biological weapons has been
in existence for a long time. There are well-established,
and in some cases very well-resourced, groups with a dem-
onstrated desire to perpetrate large-scale attacks against
civilians – and not only against developed Western states.
Both motive and opportunity appear to be in place and,
accordingly, there has been much discussion over nightmare
bioterror scenarios, with concerns (especially in the US,
but to a lesser extent in other Western countries) being
heightened after the attacks of 11 September 2001. According to this discourse, there are many plausible reasons to
presume that some terrorist groups would want to use
biological weapons, and would have the resources to acquire
them and the ability to use them. So why is the history of
actual bioterrorist attacks so slender?

Again, there are a number of potential explanations. It
could be that terrorist groups are satisfied with using other
(often much lower technology) ways of attacking their
targets. It could be (as I discuss further below) that biological weapons are in fact much harder for non-state groups
to make and use than is often supposed. It could even be
that intelligence and security services have been supremely
successful in preventing would-be bioterrorists from bringing an attack to fruition. Most likely, the truth is a combination of these factors and others. Indeed, in the
modern-day history of (bio)terrorism, there is some evidence
to support each.

In the late 1990s, it became popular to talk about the 'new' terrorism carried out by groups who were more likely to be inspired by religion rather than pursuing explicitly political aims like terrorists of the 1960s, 1970s and 1980s (e.g. Laqueur 1999). Such groups, it was said, would be more willing to carry out mass-casualty attacks and more willing to risk killing themselves in the process. They would be less amenable to negotiation with governments. Developments such as the internet and mobile communications gave them new ways to organize and prepare attacks. And the collapse of the former Soviet bloc gave them new opportunities to gain access to the materials necessary to create weapons of mass destruction (WMD) – or even to acquire ready-made WMD.

In practice, however, the terrorist attacks that have occurred to date have generally used either conventional weapons such as explosives and small arms, or have adopted novel tactics using civilian assets, as on 11 September 2001 and in the use of motor vehicles against pedestrians. Such attacks have been highly successful in drawing attention to the groups who have been responsible for carrying them out, or inspiring individuals to carry them out. In some of these attacks the death tolls have been extremely high. Public anxiety has been created and military and security forces have been put on alert. So, whilst we can't say for certain that terrorist groups will never escalate to using biological weapons or other WMD, we can at least say that they have succeeded in causing widespread fear and disruption without needing to.

The question of capability is more complex. Many terrorist organizations have access to significant resources and the 'barriers to entry' for creating biological weapons seem to be lowering. These apparently indisputable facts are the basis of many of the threat projections of counter-terrorism agencies. Recent history, however, does lend some credence to the idea that biological weapons are perhaps not as easy to successfully create and use as is often supposed. The two most high-profile bioterrorism cases of recent decades have been the (unsuccessful) attempts made by the Japanese cult Aum Shinrikyo to weaponize various pathogens; and the (much more successful) anthrax letter attacks of 2001.

Aum Shinrikyo came to public attention after it carried out a Sarin gas attack on the Tokyo subway on 20 March 1995, which killed twelve and sickened many more. Subsequent investigations into the group revealed that they had made attempts over a number of years to develop biological weapons, using pathogens including botulism and anthrax. These efforts did not meet with much success – and it was ultimately a chemical weapon attack that they perpetrated on the subway. As Sonia Ben Ouargrham-Gormley (2012) and others have argued, Aum Shinrikyo's failed efforts to create an effective biological weapon suggests that the conventional wisdom that, given access to the necessary equipment, material and scientific information, terrorist groups could develop bioweapons overlooks some of the serious practical difficulties that they would face. Not the least of these, she argues, is 'tacit knowledge' that cannot easily be translated in written form. The road from having the 'recipe' for a bioweapon to actually being able to make one can be much longer and more difficult than is often presumed. Given that even the lavishly funded Soviet and American bioweapons programmes often struggled to overcome these knowledge transfer obstacles, it is perhaps not surprising that Aum Shinrikyo failed to do so – despite having huge financial resources, and despite multiple failures by the authorities in detecting and investigating their activities (Ben Ouargrham-Gormley 2012: 99–102).

One person who did have the necessary tacit knowledge to successfully weaponize a pathogen was Bruce Ivins, the US biodefence researcher who is widely thought to be the man responsible for the 2001 anthrax letter attacks in the US, often referred to as the 'Amerithrax attacks'. On 18 September 2001, just a few days after the World Trade Center attacks, the first of a series of envelopes containing anthrax spores were mailed to US senators and news organizations. Further envelopes were mailed in early October. On 4 October, it was announced that Robert Stevens, an employee of American Media Inc. in Boca Raton, Florida, had contracted anthrax. He died the following day – the first anthrax death in the US in twenty-five years. In all, twenty-two people were infected by anthrax spores contained in at least five envelopes. Five of those people died, two of them postal workers.

As well as the anthrax spores, the envelopes included letters purporting to show an Islamic extremist motivation for the attacks. The letters sent to Senators Patrick Leahy and Thomas Daschle, for example, read:

> YOU CAN NOT STOP US.
> WE HAVE THIS ANTHRAX.
> YOU DIE NOW.
> ARE YOU AFRAID?
> DEATH TO AMERICA.
> DEATH TO ISRAEL.
> ALLAH IS GREAT.
> (US Department of Justice 2010: 2)

A major FBI-led investigation was launched, with a key breakthrough coming in 2007 when new genetic testing techniques were used to confirm that the anthrax spores used in the attacks were from a batch that had been created and maintained by Ivins as part of biodefence research at the United States Army Medical Research Institute of Infectious Diseases (USAMRIID). Ivins committed suicide in July 2008, before he could be indicted. Much of the evidence against him was released in a Department of Justice report in 2010 which concluded that 'Dr. Ivins, alone, mailed the anthrax letters' (US Department of Justice 2010: 1). Although a subsequent review of the investigation called into question the conclusiveness of the scientific evidence which had been used to identify the batch from which the spores came (National Research Council 2011), the investigation into who perpetrated the attack has not to date been re-opened.

There are a number of lessons that can be drawn from this episode. The first is that threats can come from the inside as well as the outside. Whilst much of the attention post-9/11 was on the threat posed by groups or individuals motivated by extremist versions of Islam, in this case the threat came (or, at least, the evidence suggests it came) from a white, Catholic, American scientist employed by the US Army – not where anyone was looking. This suggested there was a need to better regulate the activities of scientists involved in biodefence research and to improve security measures at government biodefence establishments, as well as to keep up surveillance efforts to identify potential bioterror threats that could be emerging almost anywhere in the world.

Whilst the scale of such a task is enough to give intelligence officials sleepless nights, there is a potentially more reassuring lesson that could be drawn from the anthrax letters case. Here was an attacker (at least, assuming Ivins was indeed the attacker) with a detailed knowledge of advanced techniques to weaponize anthrax, access to the necessary biological material and laboratory equipment, and who managed to completely evade detection in smuggling the anthrax out of his lab. Whilst it is true that the mode of his attack limited the number of people exposed to the spores (he didn't, for example, attempt to disperse it in a crowded public place), even this attacker ultimately succeeded in perpetrating only a relatively small-scale attack, one that resulted in far fewer casualties than lower-tech attacks that have used much more easily accessible vehicles, firearms or explosive devices.

Past is not always prologue. The relatively small number of previous bioterrorist attacks, and the relatively low impact of those that have been carried out, does not necessarily mean that there is no risk in future, nor that efforts shouldn't continue to prevent such risks becoming reality. But it does make it difficult to properly calibrate those efforts. How much are we prepared to invest in preventing and preparing for bioterrorist attacks of unknown likelihood? And what are the opportunity costs involved in doing so?

The huge increase in US spending on biodefence since 2001 has led to a lively debate around precisely these questions. According to *Nature*, the US government spent approximately US$60 billion on biodefence programs (including research and development efforts and the stockpiling of vaccines and other medical countermeasures) in the decade from 2001 (Check Hayden 2011). Some have argued that this investment – much of which went into scientific research on detecting, diagnosing and treating pathogens that could potentially be used by rogue states or terrorist groups – has had important knock-on benefits for public health more broadly. Burnett et al. (2005: 371), for example, have argued that 'as with all good science, many recent biodefense research discoveries/advances have also directly facilitated our understanding and ability to treat other diseases, including antibiotic resistant bacteria and viruses (such as HIV and SARS).' A study by the Center for Biosecurity at the University of Pittsburgh Medical Center found that the vast majority of US biodefence funding – $5.78 billion out of a total of $6.42 billion in FY2012 – was indeed put into programmes that 'have both biodefense and nonbiodefense goals and applications' (Franco and Sell 2011). If this research can genuinely serve routine public health as well as security goals, it could be of value even if a biological weapons attack never happens.

Others, however, have doubted whether such 'win–wins' are actually delivered in practice. Fidler and Gostin (2007) have drawn attention to the differences in the aims and approaches between the public health and security communities, pointing out amongst other things that there is a tension between security's traditional privileging of secrecy and public health's focus on scientific freedom and open dissemination of findings (an issue to which I return below). It is also unclear whether the tangible benefits for public health are in any way commensurate with the amounts spent on biodefence. For Fidler and Gostin, the real effect of the investment in research in this area has been to create and enrich a 'biodefence industrial complex' rather than bringing significant benefits for public health more broadly (Fidler and Gostin 2007).

Critics have also argued that the prioritization of programmes focusing on a narrow range of biological agents has distorted agendas and diverted attention from other naturally occurring disease threats (Scientists Working Group on Biological and Chemical Weapons 2010). As with all investments, biodefence spending clearly entails opportunity costs in that the same money cannot also be spent on other things; things that could, potentially, have a greater public health benefit. One problem with asking such a question is that we cannot assume that any money taken away from biodefence would necessarily be reallocated to another area of health; it could just as easily be used somewhere else – perhaps even in ways (for example, research into other kinds of weapons) that would be bad for health. A more immediately proximate discussion is over the extent to which biodefence spending has distorted research priorities in the life sciences. It seems logical to assume that the huge sums of money that have flowed into biodefence research (especially, but not only, in the US) will have drawn scientists' time and attention away from other things. In practice, however, some have claimed that the distorting effect has been more limited than we might initially expect. For one thing, as Judith Reppy (2008) has argued, life science research has always been heavily influenced by external funders and their priorities. The new biodefence expenditure has done little to significantly change this overall picture. And in terms of the R&D efforts of the major pharmaceutical manufacturers, Elbe, Roemer-Mahler and Long (2015) have shown that these companies have in fact had little interest in the biodefence field, where R&D costs are high and the potential markets for successful products limited, forcing the US government to create government-backed incentive schemes, and to actively support smaller biotech companies in taking biodefence research forward. Lastly, the increase in biodefence spending has come during a period in which there has been massive investment going into the life sciences in general, diluting any distorting effect that biodefence might otherwise have had. However we judge the rights and wrongs of biodefence spending (a question which is ultimately a political one), a further legitimate concern is that research in the life sciences (whether in the biodefence field or not) could pose its own biosecurity risks.

Laboratory Escapes and Scientific Misadventures

The life sciences might save us, but they might also kill us. While cases such as the anthrax letter attacks show the possibilities for the deliberate misuse of science to cause harm, the 'dual use' nature of large areas of bioscience means that even research with solely peaceful purposes can nonetheless come to represent a security risk. One of the most difficult balances to strike in this area is between preventing scientific research from causing harm, whilst at the same time avoiding unnecessarily hampering work that could deliver important health benefits. At stake here are academic freedom and scientific progress on the one hand, and the protection of populations on the other.

From Mary Shelley's *Frankenstein* onwards, there has always been suspicion, and sometimes fear, about what scientists are up to in their laboratories. Recent decades have brought huge gains in medical and biological knowledge, leading to a much greater understanding of pathogens and how humans, both individually and collectively, can be better protected against them. In some cases, however, such research has created new risks and vulnerabilities. Conducting research on preventing and treating diseases caused by deadly pathogens often involves storing and manipulating those pathogens, creating a need for stringent biosafety procedures to ensure the protection of those working in the lab – and also the public beyond the laboratory door.

Sometimes things do go wrong. Janet Parker, a medical photographer, was the last person in the world to die of smallpox. She was accidentally infected during the course of her work at Birmingham University Medical School in England, and died on 11 September 1978 – one year after the last known 'natural case' of the disease occurred in Somalia. Mrs Parker's mother also contracted smallpox from her daughter, although she fortunately recovered from her illness. Henry Bedson, Head of the Microbiology Department, committed suicide while quarantined at his home. A subsequent government-commissioned investigation into the incident (Shooter 1980[6]) made a number of criticisms of the scientists involved in the smallpox research, the University for failing to implement adequate training and safety procedures, and the government safety inspection system, which had approved the laboratory for smallpox research despite the fact that it did not meet some of the requirements of the prevailing safety code – for example, it did not have an airlock or shower and changing facilities (Shooter 1980: 42). Looking beyond the Birmingham case, the committee considered smallpox research in the UK more widely and advised that

> 11. The remaining smallpox laboratory in the United Kingdom, at St. Mary's Hospital Medical School, London, should no longer remain in a densely populated part of London. It should be re-sited in a place where facilities for containment are stringent and where the number of staff who have to be regarded as potential contacts would be smaller than in a Medical School. (Shooter 1980: 63)

As we know from the beginning of this chapter, (so far as is publicly known) no smallpox stocks now remain in the UK. But as the Bethesda incident showed, surprises can happen.

Since the 1970s, huge strides have been made in improving laboratory safety, and regulation of laboratories carrying out particularly hazardous research (at least in developed countries) has improved significantly. The CDC's 'Biosafety Level' classification system has become the *de facto* global standard, setting out requirements for laboratory facilities on a scale from BSL-1 facilities (where any research carries minimal risk of harm to humans) through to BSL-4 labs, which is 'required for work with dangerous and exotic agents that pose a high individual risk of aerosol-transmitted laboratory infections and life-threatening disease that is frequently fatal, for which there are no vaccines or treatments, or a related agent with unknown risk of transmission' (Department of Health and Human Services 2009: 45). Importantly, these biosafety regulations are not intended to prevent particular types of research being carried out; rather they are to ensure that such work is done in a way that minimizes the risks both to scientists themselves and to the wider public. They do have the effect of limiting *where* certain kinds of research can be conducted, especially research reserved for BSL-4 labs, which are not present in all countries, and remain scarce even where they do exist.[7] For the most part, scientists view biosafety regulations as an important part of professional practice rather than as a restraint on academic freedom or an impediment to scientific progress. So, whilst the need for such measures has certainly not gone away, much of the discussion has shifted from biosafety concerns (by which we mean measures to prevent unintended exposure to pathogens) and towards biosecurity concerns (defined as measures to prevent 'unauthorized access, loss, theft, misuse, diversion or intentional release') (WHO 2006: iv).

The increasing attention being paid to the threat of bioterrorism of course lies behind this. Security fears around the deliberate misuse of science have been heightened by advances in scientific capabilities – in particular the rapidly developing ability of scientists to synthetically alter and even create genetic material. The most recent high-profile development in this area at the time of writing was the successful recreation of the horsepox virus (closely related to the variola virus that causes smallpox) by Professor David Evans and his team at the University of Alberta, Canada. Although the genomic sequence of the horsepox virus (HSPV) had been published in 2006 (Tulman et al. 2006), Evans' team was the first to artificially synthesize the virus – using, as reported in *Science*, 'genetic pieces ordered in the mail' (Kupferschmidt 2017). The scientists involved in this work hoped that their breakthrough could contribute to the research and development of new and more effective vaccines. But attention naturally also turned to the potential security implications of what they had done – particularly what others might do using the same techniques. According to Gregory D. Koblentz (2017: 1), the *de novo* synthesis of horsepox crossed 'an important Rubicon in the field of biosecurity.' Without the introduction of proper safeguards, he warned, this new capability 'could provide the foundation for a disgruntled or radicalized scientist, a sophisticated terrorist group, an unscrupulous company, or a rogue state to recreate one of humanity's most feared microbial enemies' (Koblentz 2017: 2).

Is it right that such undoubtedly incredible scientific achievements should immediately give rise to security concerns rather than Nobel prizes? According to Kathleen Vogel (2013), one of the issues underlying debates in this area is the way in which we conceptualize these advances in relation to the history of bioscience research. The tendency of security and intelligence agencies to see such developments as a revolutionary (as in the crossing of a Rubicon) rather than an evolutionary change in scientific research, she argues, can lead to them overestimating the risks, and failing to incorporate into their risk assessments some of the broader contextual factors which could 'lead to fundamentally different conclusions about the character and trajectory of biotechnology developments and their implications for bioweapons threats' (Vogel 2013: 44). As with the discussion in the previous section on the importance of tacit knowledge to successful bioweapons development, Vogel highlights the broader social aspects of successful research and development in synthetic biology, pointing to the requirements for particular kinds of tacit 'know how', and the existence of 'bottlenecks' in the process of diffusing findings in a way that can be reliably replicated elsewhere. In addition, she argues that a broad range of political, economic and regulatory contextual factors have a significant impact on knowledge diffusion and translation (Vogel 2014). In short, assuming that the ability of one group of highly-trained scientists to synthesize a particular genetic sequence, whether of horsepox or something else, will lead inevitably to other groups (perhaps more careless ones, or perhaps ill-intentioned ones) being able to repeat the trick causes us, according to Vogel, to overestimate the severity of the threat.

Whether or not research that has potential biosecurity implications should be published openly in academic journals – and thus potentially made available to terrorists – has been another topic of concern in recent years, with the work of Ron Fouchier and colleagues at the Rotterdam Medical Centre and Yoshihiro Kawaoka and colleagues at the University of Wisconsin-Madison becoming a lightning rod for debate between proponents of biosecurity and defenders of academic freedom (see Enemark 2017: 80–9). Both of these labs were carrying out so-called 'gain of function' experiments in which they were modifying influenza viruses in order to make them transmissible through the air (in the experiments the viruses were being passed between ferrets, although potentially they would also pass between humans) and to make them more virulent. The controversy centred on whether research articles describing the process through which the teams had modified the flu viruses should be openly published. The US National Science Advisory Board for Biosecurity (NSABB) initially ruled that they should not, citing the risk that the knowledge contained in the articles could be misused by terrorists looking to produce a dangerous weapon,[8] and also arguing that decisions on these issues should not be left to scientists alone, but should be made with input from biosecurity experts (Osterholm and

Olshaker 2017). Prior to publication, the NSABB decided that information from the articles should be redacted to reduce the security risk. In response to protests from scientists and the NIH, the US government asked the NSABB to reconsider. In its second vote on the issue, the NSABB agreed that the studies could be published, which they subsequently were in *Science* (Herfst et al. 2012) and *Nature* (Imai et al. 2012), respectively.

Michael T. Osterholm, a member of the NSABB in favour of requiring redaction of the articles, has continued to argue for the need to limit the circulation of security-sensitive knowledge of this type. Writing in 2017, he argued that

> The answer is clear. We need to do these studies in a few select labs with leading experts and state-of-the-art safety features. And this research needs to be classified – or at least considered sensitive – so that the results are shared only with those who need to know. We can support the US government and other responsible governments of the world in anticipating and preparing for potential microbe-related threats with this approach. (Osterholm and Olshaker 2017)

But not all agree. How the correct balance between the risks and benefits of publishing such research should be struck continues to be debated. The open dissemination of scientific findings is at the very heart of the scientific method, allowing other researchers to replicate the original experiment and confirm (or disprove) its findings, as well as to build on them in future research. At one level, then, we might want to take the position that any limitation on a scientist's ability to publish the results of her research undermines the scientific method, and thus potentially hinders scientific progress. In this particular case, those involved in the research made the argument that this kind of experiment was particularly important given that influenza viruses naturally mutate, and that the mutations deliberately created in the lab were ones which could conceivably happen 'in the wild'. Thus, this scientific work could help us better understand natural changes in viruses that can lead to the emergence of new pandemic strains, and also allow us to be better prepared to defend against them – for example, by developing new vaccines. Far from being a security threat, this type of research, according to this argument, could actually increase our security against a future pandemic.

As Casadevall and Imperiale (2014) argued, the calculation of risks and benefits in this case ultimately comes down to a judgement call, in which the assessment is severely hampered by limited information. We can't quantify the likelihood of an accidental release of a pathogen as a result of this kind of research, nor of an individual or group attempting (still less succeeding) in using this knowledge for nefarious purposes. On the benefits side, the potential future scientific value of these experiments, which could be built upon by others in ways that are potentially unforeseeable at the current time, is similarly difficult to calculate. Such experiments could lead to hugely beneficial scientific advances. Then again, they might not.

Faced with such uncertainties, the natural inclination of security policymakers is often to proceed on the basis of worst-case scenarios, to want to limit the dissemination of 'dual use' knowledge and to strictly regulate the circumstances in which such work can be done (if at all). This trend was apparent long before the Fouchier and Kawaoka cases, for example in the attempts by the US Department of Defense in 2002 to put greater restrictions on the publication of Pentagon-funded research – a move that was strongly opposed by US universities and researchers (Malakoff 2002). Interestingly, this opposition was not only on the grounds of academic freedom (although that was an important part of it), but it was also argued that the proposed regulations could in fact be self-defeating, further discouraging engagement in these programmes 'just as world-class researchers and companies were showing greater interest in doing defense research' (Jacques Gansler, quoted in Malakoff 2002).[9]

If it is difficult for security policymakers to find an effective way of calculating the risks and benefits of particular types of bioscience research, it is perhaps even harder for individual scientists to do so. In 2001, there was controversy over the publication of a paper by a group of Australian researchers who had unintentionally created a vaccine-resistant and lethal (to mice) form of mousepox virus. The researchers involved had little awareness at the time of any potential security implications of their research, nor did they have ready access to advice on these issues. As Ronald Jackson, one of the researchers, said, 'The reality was that there was no one there to advise us. This was all before September 11, 2001' (quoted in Selgelid and Weir 2010: 20). No potential security concerns with publishing the research were noted during the peer review process (indeed, as Jackson reports it, 'The referees' reports said that this was a fairly mundane paper and they were dubious whether they should publish it or not', quoted in Selgelid and Weir 2010: 21). It was only when a story focusing on the research emerged in *The New Scientist* (Nowak 2001) that the experiment came to be politically controversial, seen as exemplifying the dilemma of 'How do you stop terrorists taking legitimate research and adapting it for their own nefarious purposes?'

For Selgelid, awareness-raising amongst scientists cannot be a complete solution to this problem: there will always be some limitations on what we can expect scientists to foresee as a result of the secrecy of much of the intelligence on which a proper assessment of risk rests. In the mousepox case, for example, he argues that

> Assessing the security risks of the mousepox publication requires knowledge about the likely proliferation of the smallpox virus (e.g. from alleged former Soviet bioweapons stockpiles) because would-be bioterrorists would need to have access to the smallpox virus to apply the mousepox genetic engineering technique to it (if their aim is to produce vaccine-resistant smallpox). Detailed information about the likelihood of smallpox proliferation, however, is classified information held by intelligence and security experts (if anyone). In the case of the mousepox study, scientists (lacking

security clearance) are systematically denied access to information essential to assessment of the security risks of the relevant publication. (Selgelid 2008: 721)

Whilst such informational deficiencies may make it difficult for researchers to come to fully informed judgements about the potential biosecurity risks of their research, dual-use education could at least help sensitize them to the issues and lead them to seek guidance. The need for such education has been recognized within the BWC process since 2003, although implementation of education programmes has been slow (Nixdorff 2013). Those who have been directly involved in work to educate scientists on these issues have often found low levels of awareness, and large disparities in education and training between different national contexts (e.g. Revill et al. 2012).

Clearly raising the knowledge and awareness of scientists about the potential biosecurity (and not merely biosafety) implications of their work cannot be a bad thing, but it is doubtful whether this is in itself enough to ensure an adequate balance is struck between security and scientific freedom. This is where the politics inevitably comes in. In the absence of the ability to fully quantify risks and benefits, political choices need to be made about the government's (and, by extension, the public's) appetite for risk on the one hand, and the value of open science on the other. As I argue in the conclusion to this chapter, professional scientists are important participants in this debate, in particular in defending the value of open science and academic freedom over the tendency of security policymakers to prefer a 'play it safe' approach.

Homebrew Biotechnology

If knowledge about biosecurity concerns is limited amongst professional scientists, what can we realistically expect of amateur 'citizen scientists'? This has become a live issue in recent years in the field of synthetic biology in particular, where technological advances are lowering some of the barriers to entry. What some see as the resultant 'de-skilling' has led to a heightening of security concerns, a significant portion of which have been directed at so-called 'DIY biology'. The DIY biology movement (DIYbio – see, for example, DIYbio.org), which frequently explicitly likens itself to the 'maker' and computer hacker communities (and indeed sometimes uses the phrase 'biohacking') focuses its efforts on the development of 'open source' science and the sharing of knowledge. For those in the DIYbio community, many of whom have significant scientific expertise, even if they are often dismissed as amateur hobbyists, the movement offers the potential for scientific breakthroughs to be made at low cost, and in ways that can maximize access to the benefits (for example, by avoiding the strong patent protections on which commercial R&D-based organizations such as pharmaceutical companies rely) (e.g. Nature 2013). DIYbio also opens up exciting new research possibilities, including collaborations between 'professional' and 'amateur' scientists (Landrain et al. 2013).

For security policymakers, however, this community can be seen as a new source of threat, as amateur 'garage biologists' 'play around' with modifying viruses and bacteria, potentially without the necessary skills and training to do so safely – and certainly without the level of biosafety that is required in BSL-3 and BSL-4 labs (Department of Health and Human Services 2009). Even worse, some of those in the DIYbio community could misuse their new-found knowledge to cause harm, or could unwittingly pave the way for others to use their research as the basis for deliberate attacks. Ronald K. Noble, then-Secretary-General of Interpol, argued that

> during the last few years, biological agents have increasingly been used in nefarious ways by individuals who did not belong to any specific terrorist or criminal organization. This worrying trend collides with the emerging concept of

'do-it-yourself biology,' or DIYbio, an 'open science' movement whose proponents believe that scientific innovation,
technology, and research should be available to all inquiring
minds, be they amateurs or professionals, inside or outside
traditional laboratories. Although DIYbio's cross-disciplinary
practitioners, including citizen scientists such as amateur
bioengineers and biologists, have developed an operating
principle of 'no pathogens and no bioweapons,' this new
context of scientific research and development could lead
to an infinite variety of potential dual-use biotechnologies
that could eventually be misused. (Noble 2013: 50)

Again, here we come up against two questions that have
already been confronted in this chapter, albeit accompanied
by a narrative that presupposes a higher degree of risk as
a result of the 'amateur' status of members of the DIYbio
movement. These questions are, first, what is the likelihood
of such citizen scientists in fact wanting or being able to
create pathogens of significant security concern? And, second,
how can their activities best be regulated in order to strike
an acceptable balance between security concerns and the
advancement of science?

In terms of the former, once again arguments around
tacit knowledge have been put forward to challenge the
doomsday scenarios that some have set out. Just as with
bioterrorism, it has been argued that viewing DIYbio as a
significant security threat rests upon some dubious assumptions about the apparent accessibility of sophisticated bioscience techniques and the supposed ease of engineering
pathogens of security concern. Jefferson, Lentzos and Marris
(2014), for example, have argued that proponents of the
DIYbio threat narrative understate the costs and practical
difficulty of performing some of the techniques that are
often claimed to be accessible to amateur scientists; underestimate the expertise and skill of many members of the
DIYbio community; ignore the fact that in reality even
highly sophisticated laboratories have rarely succeeded in
'designing' new pathogens; and overestimate the scale of
the threat, both because there is little evidence that

would-be terrorists see biological weapons as a preferred form of mass-casualty attack, and secondly because of the extreme difficulties (seen above in the case of Aum Shinrikyo) of making the step from having pathogenic material to creating an effective weapon.

The difficulty with such arguments is that they are inevitably vulnerable to projections of future technological developments. Even if it is true that the likelihood of a skilled 'homebrew biologist' succeeding in creating a viable biological weapon is currently low, it is difficult to disprove the idea that the threat will increase over time as the necessary technologies become cheaper and easier to use. CRISPR gene editing technology, for example, has attracted attention in recent years as a powerful tool for quickly, easily and (relatively) cheaply altering the DNA of an organism (Ledford 2015). Bill Gates (2018) has argued that CRISPR could even 'transform global development'. But it has also attracted attention from the intelligence community: in 2016, prompted by the developments in CRISPR technology the previous year, the potential threat of genome editing was added to the US intelligence community's 'Worldwide Threat Assessment' for the first time (Clapper 2016: 9; see also Regalado 2016). The World Economic Forum included 'advances such as artificial intelligence, geo-engineering and synthetic biology causing human, environmental and economic damage' in its 2017 *Global Risks Report* (WEF 2017). It is difficult to argue against the view that as CRISPR and other gene editing technologies become cheaper, it may only be a matter of time before experiments that are currently out of reach of the average DIYbio enthusiast (either because of cost or a lack of the necessary tacit knowledge) may one day become possible.

To the objection that there is little reason to think that would-be terrorists have any desire to pursue such weapons, proponents of the security threat narrative are able to point to the inherent uncertainties in assessing the likely intentions of future terrorist groups; the possibility that individuals may be capable of carrying out such activities alone; and the risk that even well-intentioned DIYbio activities could lead to the accidental release of dangerous pathogens. These types of concerns have tended to shift the debate onto the terrain of regulation.

But how can regulation effectively reduce the potential future risks from DIYbio or similar movements? Attempting to limit access to particular technologies is one obvious option, but one that few believe is likely to be effective. Elsewhere there have been calls for gene editing to be added to the Biological Weapons Convention, for increased global surveillance to identify potential sources of threat, and for the (US) Dual-Use Research of Concern Policy to be broadened to apply to small labs and individuals (Gerstein 2016). On the other side of the debate, Robert Carlson, to take one example, has argued that 'Proscription of information and artifacts generally leads to a black market that is difficult to monitor and therefore difficult to police. A superior alternative is the deliberate creation of an open and expansive research community, which may be better able to respond to crises and better able to keep track of research whether in the university or the garage' (Carlson 2003: 203).

As with professional scientists, one set of possible responses – and some argue the most likely to be effective – are around education and self-regulation of DIYbio enthusiasts. Encouragingly, there is already strong evidence from within the DIYbio community of an acute awareness of the need to ensure that its work is carried out safely and in a manner that minimizes security risks. Indeed, in some respects it may be true to say that there has been *more* awareness and emphasis of these risks amongst 'amateur' enthusiasts in the DIYbio movement than amongst some professional scientists in universities and research institutes. As early as 1975, researchers in the emerging field of DNA recombinant technology met at the Asilomar Conference to discuss and create guidelines for responsible research conduct. Now, the DIYbio.org site includes codes of ethics,[10] offers expert advice on biosafety,[11] and features lengthy discussion threads on a wide range of biosafety and bios-ecurity topics. No doubt some of the impetus for these attempts at self-regulation comes from a desire to avoid restrictive governmental regulations being placed upon them. Whilst such attempts to regulate may well come in future (particularly if there are any incidents that governments feel forced to respond to), thus far the security community in the US (where this debate is by far the most advanced) have shown a willingness to pursue a strategy of educating 'amateur biologists' and other 'non-traditional audiences' on dual-use issues (e.g. NSABB 2010: 12; 2011).

Whatever the strategy adopted in future, it would clearly be impossible to completely remove any element of risk from DIYbio, again requiring a political balance to be struck between security and other social goods. This includes not only the freedom of 'amateur' biologists to pursue their hobby, but also the potential scientific gains that might arise from their research. But just as with professional labs, quantifying the potential benefit is an impossible task, while merely the prospect of a potential risk, however remote, may be enough to make security-concerned governments feel that they need to take tough action.

Conclusion

The questions that governments confront are not whether biosciences potentially represent a security threat (poten-tially, they do), but how much security do we want, and what are we prepared to sacrifice in order to get it?

Making good policy in a situation of massive uncertainty is always a fearsomely difficult task, but it is the task that faces governments in responding to all of the issues that have been looked at in this chapter. From the perspective of a security policymaker, a precautionary approach may well seem to be the most politically attractive. But the cons of such an approach can also be real – in terms of oppor-tunity costs, both economically and scientifically, but also in terms of scientific freedoms. It is too simplistic to view scientists and security policymakers as being on opposite ends of the spectrum in these policy dilemmas (after all, many scientists are also engaged in security policymaking – including around biological weapons and biodefence programmes), but at the same time it is true that to some extent the interests of science and those of security are sometimes pulling in opposite directions.

Security would be expected to be prioritized by governments facing such a choice – and as we have seen in this chapter, often it is. Governments invest in biodefence efforts, seek to prevent would-be bioterrorists being able to create and use biological weapons, and worry about how they can best regulate scientists, both 'professional' and 'amateur'. But this prioritization is a political choice – and a topic of ongoing debate. Scientists concerned about the negative impacts that security policies can have on their work have been active participants in that debate, arguing for the value of open science and the fundamental principles of the scientific method. Sometimes these arguments have won out. These debates are likely to get more complex over the coming years as scientific and technological progress opens up new potential sources of both opportunity and threat. A major bioterrorist incident could alter the current balance dramatically, making governments favour tighter restrictions and tougher regulations, whether scientists like it or not.

So complex is the science involved in fields such as DNA synthesis and gene editing that few members of the general public can grasp the intricacies of what is being done, nor can they be expected to be able to adequately weigh up the pros and cons for themselves. This makes it more important than ever that those involved in the biosciences are educated and conversant in both the biosafety and the biosecurity aspects of this research. This education is not only important, as is often presumed, in making scientists think twice before beginning work with potential security implications. It is also important in better equipping them for being active participants in debates over risks and benefits. Unless the case for open science is put forcefully and convincingly, with its benefits fully explained to governments and the public, security concerns are likely to win out, and we may ultimately find that we have sacrificed more than we realized in the pursuit of greater, although perhaps still elusive, security.

In thinking about pathogen-related scientific research as a potential threat to health security, we find a different relationship between disease and security than we saw in chapters 1 and 2, and a different set of mitigation measures available to governments. Rather than dealing with 'natural' outbreaks, the man-made nature of the threats discussed in this chapter adds a further level of uncertainty; uncertainty about human intentions, and uncertainty about the direction future technological developments will take. Regulating these sources of risk – what happens in labs, and how scientific knowledge is shared – is a very different one than trying to regulate the movement of pathogens. It also throws up very different political issues. In the next three chapters, attention shifts to the political consequences of the securitization processes that we have seen so far in the book, beginning with a discussion of what securitization has meant for human rights and civil liberties.

– 4 –

Disease, Human Rights and Security Responses

On 11 November 1938, Mary Mallon died, having spent the last 23 years of her life incarcerated for the protection of the public's health. 'Typhoid Mary', as she became widely known, was the source of a series of typhoid outbreaks in New York in the early twentieth century. Working as a cook in the homes of wealthy families, Mallon was ideally positioned to spread the disease, of which she was an asymptomatic carrier. Becoming infamous as 'the most deadly cook in America' (Campbell Bartoletti 2015), and remaining a byword to this day for an individual who brings death and destruction to a community, Mallon was quarantined on two occasions, both times against her strongly expressed wishes. After the first incarceration (1907–10) she was released on the promise that she would stop working as a cook – a promise on which she later reneged, leading to a second spell in enforced quarantine that lasted the remainder of her life, from 1915 to 1938.

Mallon's case is a prime example of the fact that public health policies often involve making trade-offs between the protection of the public from disease threats and the rights and liberties of individuals who may be carriers of a disease. There is a long history of attempts to properly strike this balance. There is an equally long history of rights abuses in the name of public health that seem shocking to modern sensibilities. Yet even in contemporary outbreak crises, we have seen many instances in which the theoretical safeguards have been ignored and people's rights have been trampled on. This might tell us something important about the ways in which rights and security considerations are ranked (at least by some governments) in emergency situations.

That securitization can lead to anti-democratic responses, often ones that undermine human rights and civil liberties, is one of the most well-rehearsed arguments of securitization sceptics. We have seen this dynamic play out in the 'War on Terror' and the 'War on Drugs', among many other examples. It is one of the main reasons that the Copenhagen School expresses a preference for desecuritization and for addressing societal challenges within the realm of 'normal' politics rather than the emergency modalities of security (Buzan, Waever and de Wilde 1998; Hansen 2012). As I argued in the Introduction, however, this distinction between security politics and normal politics is not as stark as securitization theorists often suggest, and in practice perceived threats occupy a variety of positions on the spectrum between the two. The balancing of security and rights is dynamic – and it is contested.

In this chapter, I examine the trade-offs that are often made between security from disease and the rights of individuals not to face discrimination or other curtailments of their liberties. In the first section, building on the discussions in chapter 1, I look at how these trade-offs play out at the border; and in the second section at domestic practices of outbreak response, looking at common forms of health security policy in relation to the Siracusa Principles, which are supposed to guide governments who seek to derogate from civil and political rights during an emergency. Although rights often come off poorly in these cases, I argue that the apparent conflict between public health and human rights is not so binary as is often supposed, and that there are even circumstances in which curtailing rights in the name of security might actually lead to *less* public health security, not more.

In the third part of the chapter, I examine the idea that we could reconceptualize this debate in terms of a conflict of rights, rather than a case of rights versus security. On the one hand, according to this view, we have the contagious individual, who has rights. On the other, we must consider the right to health of the wider population, which must also be protected. Does this make it any easier for us to find a way through the impasse? Unfortunately not, for two main reasons. First, it is less than clear what the right to health actually entails. Second, the right to health, like other social and economic rights, is a weak claim in many places. Many governments do not see the right to health as placing particular obligations on them, meaning that it is unable to compete with the security discourse that views infectious individuals as a threat to the body politic.

I conclude the chapter by looking ahead to chapter 5, arguing that there is a need in political discussions of public health security and human rights not only to consider individual rights in the classic liberal conception, but also to address structures of discrimination and marginalization that frequently shape emergency responses. It may not have been coincidental to Mary Mallon's treatment by the authorities that she was an Irish immigrant – a group heavily discriminated against in New York of the early twentieth century. Typhoid Mary's misfortune was that she was seen *both* as a threat to public health *and* as coming from the 'wrong' social background. The long history of disease outbreaks being (rightly or wrongly) associated with particular social groups persists to this day – and rarely in ways that advantage the under-privileged.

Disease, Security, Borders and Rights

We have already seen the emergence of a prominent and powerful narrative around the insecurity generated by the cross-border spread of disease in a globalized world. According to this narrative, the contemporary infectious individual represents an even greater threat than Mary Mallon did. Today's disease carrier can be the source of an outbreak that not only affects the community in which she lives, but potentially the entire world.

The search for 'patient zero' has become a routine part of the public health and media response to outbreaks (Wald 2008) – and often a prominent feature of attempts to learn lessons in the aftermath of major public health emergencies. The West African Ebola outbreak of 2014–16 was no exception. Once the scale of the outbreak began to be recognized, attention quickly turned to trying to trace its origins. The person generally identified as the first human case in the outbreak was a two-year-old boy living in the village of Meliandou in rural Guinea (I am deliberately not naming him here, although he was widely named in media reports). Many suspect that he somehow came into contact with a bat, which are known animal reservoirs of the Ebola virus (e.g. Saéz et al. 2014). Whether or not that suspicion is correct, the human tragedy and the 'threat to regional and global security' – in the words of then-US President Barack Obama addressing the UN Security Council (Obama 2014a) – came together in the body of an innocent toddler. As *The Guardian* reported the case, 'Ebola turned a Guinean family tragedy into a west African crisis' (Ní Chonghaile 2014).

The unfortunate 'patient zero' in the West African Ebola outbreak had died long before he was identified. He could scarcely be blamed for having contracted the disease, nor for having transmitted it to others. Yet in other epidemics, the politics of blame comes quickly to the fore as individual disease carriers become viewed as perpetrators of reckless or even mendacious actions that put the health of others at risk. Mary Mallon was certainly viewed in this way, as was Gaétan Dugas, who we met in chapter 2. Thomas Duncan, who travelled from Liberia to Texas during the West African Ebola outbreak and was the source of a small number of infections in the United States, was too. He was heavily criticized for (apparently) providing misleading information before boarding a flight in Monrovia, thereby creating an unacceptable risk for others – not only his fellow passengers on board the aircraft, but also the medical staff who treated him after he became ill in Dallas (e.g. Onishi and Santora 2014). In the UK, meanwhile, Scottish nurse Pauline Cafferkey, who contracted Ebola virus disease whilst working in an Ebola treatment unit in Sierra Leone, faced an investigation over whether she had deliberately sought to avoid her infection being detected at Heathrow Airport on her return to the UK. The Independent Panel that investigated her actions ultimately concluded that they did not amount to professional misconduct (Nursing and Midwifery Council 2016). Even so, the damage to her reputation was done, and during the investigation she was widely portrayed in the media as someone who had put the nation's health at risk through attempting to conceal her high temperature during the entry screening process (e.g. Stewart 2016).

When it is said that 'pathogens know no borders', what is really meant is that their hosts cross those borders. Sometimes those disease hosts are animals, at other times diseases can be imported in food that is being traded between countries. More commonly in the public imagination, however, it is individual human carriers of a disease that are responsible for cross-border contagion. But whilst pathogens themselves may not recognize borders, in most places the people who are carrying them experience borders as a very real phenomenon indeed. For security policymakers, the border is a key site at which attempts can be made to intercept incoming security threats. This certainly includes pathogens – despite the rhetorical acceptance that *cordons sanitaires* can never be completely effective in a globalized world.

As well as being sites for the (attempted) interception of incoming diseases, borders are often danger zones more generally when it comes to abuses of human rights and civil liberties. Few areas are more heavily securitized than borders – especially airports. Undocumented migrants, to take one group, are routinely exposed to rights abuses at the border in many jurisdictions, and in some cases supposed health security fears have played a part in this – even in democratic societies. What is more, this has not only been seen in cases of rapidly spreading pandemics of the type we looked at in chapter 1, but also HIV. The US's treatment of Haitian refugees suspected of being HIV+ during the early 1990s is perhaps the most notorious example. Around 260–270 Haitian refugees who had tested positive for HIV were segregated at Camp Bulkeley at the US Naval Base in Guantanamo Bay – a 'liminal zone' in terms of US territory. The detainees were surrounded by barbed wire fences and guarded by the Marine Corps, since they were deemed to pose a risk to the safety of the US population – even though HIV was already well-established within the US, and had been for well over a decade. The forced detention finally came to an end after it was ruled by a US court to be both unconstitutional and contrary to international law (Johnson 1994: 305). In the intervening years, Guantanamo has occupied a far more high-profile place in the US's security policy and has again attracted the ire of human rights campaigners (e.g. Ratner 2003). But as Andrea Field (2012) has argued, 'Camp Bulkeley is a valuable part of Guantánamo's past because it moves the debate about the U.S. government's role in national security beyond terrorism to issues surrounding public health and individual rights.'

One of the main justifications for the holding of PLWHA at Camp Bulkeley was the US immigration regulations of the time, which declared that PLWHA were inadmissible for entry into the country without being specifically granted a waiver. In other words, the detention of the Haitian refugees was an extreme manifestation of a more generalized policy position. This immigration regulation, on the face of it highly discriminatory and stigmatizing, was usually justified by its supporters on two grounds. The first was public health, in particular a purported concern for ensuring the security of the US population against the importation of disease. As the high-profile conservative commentator Pat Buchanan put it, 'Why would you knowingly bring into this country hundreds and hundreds of people who are carriers of this infection and who could pass it on and kill American citizens?' (cited in Quereshi 1995: 100). The second common justification was an economic argument: that the long-term costs of providing the necessary treatment and care for PLWHA would be a burden upon the nation's resources, with some being concerned that 'people from around the world might try to get residence in the U.S. in order to get treatment' (Laurence Farer, cited in Allin 1988: 1055).

The US was certainly not the only country to apply such restrictions, which came to be heavily criticized by the global AIDS community, including by international institutions such as UNAIDS and the Global Fund (Rushton 2012). In a concerted effort to persuade countries to remove such restrictions, UNAIDS stressed the human rights case for doing so, but also highlighted their ineffectiveness. Indeed, they argued that such restrictions on movement could actually be counter-productive as 'those who are concerned they might be infected will take steps to avoid detection and will avoid contact with health and social services' (Mann 1988: 9–10). A 2006 survey of 1100 PLWHA who travelled from the UK to the USA found that a majority in practice travelled to the USA illegally (i.e. without a waiver, and without declaring their HIV sero-status) and that, fearing that discovery of antiretroviral medications in their luggage would lead to them being denied entry, a significant minority stopped their treatment for the duration of their visit (Mahto et al. 2006). Ironically, given that protecting public health was used to justify the entry restrictions, Mahto et al. (2006: 204) argued that such unplanned interruptions to treatment posed a public health risk through the potential development of drug resistance. Here we find a clear example of regulations that do not effectively balance health security concerns (however misplaced) with human rights, but rather undermine both.

The US eventually removed its HIV travel restrictions in 2010, although similar rules remain in place elsewhere. But requirements for health declarations in respect of a wide range of other infectious diseases are commonplace in many countries' visa and immigration procedures, and carrying a serious infectious disease (or being unable to prove that you do not) is often a valid reason for refusing entry. As we saw in chapter 1, during acute outbreak emergencies, such border controls are often stepped up. Despite committing under the International Health Regulations to only apply travel restrictions in cases where they are necessary and recommended by the WHO, governments frequently implement them in emergencies, even if doing so is contrary to WHO advice. I argued in chapter 1 that, from the perspective of a security policymaker who sees an overseas outbreak as a threat to the nation's security, such travel bans are perhaps understandable. Again, Ebola is a useful example: the outbreak was highly concentrated in only three countries but there was public fear of the arrival of the Ebola virus in many nations, and governments were under pressure to take (and, perhaps equally importantly, be seen to take) action to protect their populations – making domestic politics a key determinant of the likelihood of barriers being imposed (Worsnop 2017). Travel bans were a natural response to domestic political pressure.

It is notable, however, that much of the criticism of border restrictions in the Ebola case focused on the practical reasons for opposing travel bans: the fact that they were ineffective, hampered the response effort and undermined the global health security regime. Human rights considerations were a less common basis of critique, probably reflecting the view that effective disease control was a stronger political argument than human rights – especially during what was being seen as a potential global crisis. But travel and trade bans – as well as other forms of health screening at the border – do not only limit the movement of people infected with a disease, but also those that raise suspicions of being potentially infected. In practice, this can lead to stigma and discrimination against people who fit the profile of a 'disease carrier' – for example, when individuals from particular regions or ethnic groups are subject to more intrusive forms of screening, whether or not they are at genuine risk of carrying a disease (Aiello 2014).

Human Rights, the Siracusa Principles and Domestic Outbreak Response

The border is not the only place where rights abuses happen, of course: governments' domestic responses, targeted at their own citizens, can often be injurious to rights and liberties too. Neither are governments of the Global North the only ones guilty of trampling on rights and liberties in the name of health security during outbreak emergencies. Far from it.

The International Health Regulations say that they should be implemented 'with full respect for the dignity, human rights and fundamental freedoms of persons.' However, they give little guidance as to precisely what that means in practice (Zidar 2015). For that we must look elsewhere. Recognizing that trade-offs sometimes have to be made, the Siracusa Principles (American Association for the International Commission of Jurists 1985) were intended to address the problem that security concerns, particularly in the context of acute emergencies, were frequently cited by governments as justification for imposing martial law, or introducing other restrictions on people's rights that are guaranteed under the International Covenant on Civil and Political Rights (ICCPR). Developed by a panel of international lawyers, they seek to set out the circumstances under which derogations of rights can be legitimate, and the kinds of procedural safeguards that should be put in place. The Siracusa Principles are of interest to those concerned with health and human rights because, as we have already seen, public health emergencies frequently see governments taking actions that infringe on rights covered in the ICCPR on the grounds of the protection of public health and national security (Amon 2014). The principles do recognize that this can be a valid justification, noting in paragraph 25 that

> 25. Public health may be invoked as a ground for limiting certain rights in order to allow a state to take measures dealing with a serious threat to the health of the population or individual members of the population. These measures must be specifically aimed at preventing disease or injury or providing care for the sick and injured.

But they set out a number of considerations for governments derogating from rights in the case of a 'public emergency' (which, for our purposes here, means a disease-related public emergency). These include, in summary:

- that there be an 'exceptional and actual or imminent danger which threatens the life of the nation';
- that the state of emergency must be officially declared, according to national legal procedures;
- that the derogation measures are 'strictly necessary';
- that they are the least restrictive means possible in order to achieve the goal;
- that they are based on scientific evidence;
- that some rights cannot be derogated from, whatever the emergency;[12] and
- that the measures be effective in reducing the danger.

Notwithstanding the fact that these principles are amenable to obvious debates over matters of interpretation, and that they do not have the status of international law (and are in any case unenforceable), they do nevertheless provide a useful normative yardstick against which to judge the legitimacy of government actions during disease outbreak emergencies. In practice, perhaps unsurprisingly, when judged against such standards, the actions of governments are frequently found wanting.

There is a wide range of domestic emergency measures that governments put in place in response to disease crises, from large-scale social interventions such as closing schools and transport systems, to medical interventions such as mass vaccination campaigns, through to more individually targeted measures such as mandatory quarantine. Each of these, to different extents, raises issues that relate directly to the human rights and civil liberties of individuals – and which can therefore be judged according to the Siracusa Principles.

The actions of the Canadian authorities during the 2003 SARS outbreak are an instructive case in point. SARS, discussed in chapter 1, was a new, deadly, airborne disease that created concern for public health worldwide – not least in Toronto, the most affected city outside of Asia. Toronto implemented a massive quarantine operation, on a scale far beyond that of other cities with similarly sized outbreaks. Some 30,000 people were quarantined in Toronto, approximately 100 people for every confirmed SARS case, in comparison to Beijing, which quarantined twelve people for every case – a figure that was itself criticized for being over-zealous (Schabas 2004). Given that quarantine involves severe restrictions being placed on the liberties of people who may or may not be infected with the disease in question, what can we make of these actions by a liberal democracy that has traditionally been an outspoken advocate of human rights (Lui 2012)? Why did the authorities in Toronto choose to strike the balance between security and rights in this way? And did they get it right?

Politically, again it is easy to understand why the authorities wanted to take a cautious approach in such circumstances. The dual advantages here were of quelling public fears and avoiding potential criticism for having under-reacted. In such a rapidly developing outbreak situation, it could be argued that the Siracusa Principles, while nice in theory, are just too difficult to implement in practice – especially in the case of an emerging infectious disease. There was limited scientific evidence on key aspects of the

SARS virus and its epidemiology and a lack of clarity over the effectiveness of different types of public health response (including quarantine). With the benefit of hindsight, we know that precautionary quarantine was not a particularly effective intervention in the SARS case (since it is not infectious until symptoms are apparent), and that other cities that took a different approach fared at least as well as Toronto (Schabas 2004). In Siracusa Principles terms, there are real questions, then, over proportionality, evidence and effectiveness, even though the quarantine measures were legal, although that judgement rests at least to some extent on the benefit of hindsight.

In Toronto's favour is the fact that their quarantine arrangements were largely voluntary. This was not a case of 30,000 people being incarcerated against their will. People suspected of having been exposed to the virus were encouraged to submit to voluntary quarantine, mostly at home, for the good of themselves and others. Only in twenty-nine cases of non-compliance with such requests were legal quarantine orders made. To some extent this might be seen to mitigate the impact on human rights and civil liberties, given that people were largely not compelled. But 'voluntariness' certainly doesn't remove rights concerns entirely. As Lesley Jacobs (2007: 526) has argued, there are real question marks over the extent to which consent to quarantine can really be considered 'voluntary' given the imbalances in power and knowledge between public health authorities and ordinary members of the public – and the fact that the requests for cooperation were ultimately backed by legal compulsion where necessary. Exactly why Toronto made the choices it did is not entirely clear, even years after the event. By most accounts, the adoption and implementation of the policy did not involve anything resembling a detailed analysis of the ways in which individual rights and public health/security were being balanced:

> The picture ... that emerges about quarantine decisions in Ontario is one of arbitrariness and little due process.

> There is no public record of senior public health officials
> consulting with either the Ontario Human Rights Commis-
> sion nor the Ontario Privacy Commissioner about rights
> setting boundaries on the nature of imposing quarantine
> orders nor in interviews that I conducted in Toronto does
> anyone recollect any such consultations. ...Moreover, the
> record is one of disregard of such concerns about the use
> of quarantines, even when those concerns were raised by
> other medical officers outside the public health field. (Jacobs
> 2007: 534)

Notwithstanding the doubts about the extent to which
quarantine can truly have been said to be voluntary, for
the most part in Toronto compliance was not legally or
physically coerced. But this is certainly not always the case
when quarantine is enacted – even outside of large-scale
outbreaks. The case of Andrew Speaker again highlighted
the complex trade-offs to be made between individual rights
and liberties and the protection of public health – in this
instance around the forcible isolation of a US citizen believed
to be infected with extensively-drug resistant tuberculosis
(XDR-TB) (Enemark 2017: 115–16; Markel, Gostin and
Fidler 2007). Speaker was abroad on his honeymoon in
Greece when he was contacted by the US CDC, who
informed him that he had XDR-TB and should not travel
in case he transmitted the infection to others. Speaker defied
this advice, and evaded a request for border agents to identify and detain him by flying to Canada and driving across
the border to the US. Once the CDC had tracked him
down, a federal isolation order was issued requiring him
to remain under medical isolation. This attracted attention
because it was so unusual – the first case of such an order
for some fifty years (Markel, Gostin and Fidler 2007: 83)
– but also because of public and media outrage over what
were seen as Speaker's irresponsible actions in risking the
spread of such a dangerous drug-resistant form of TB. As
Parmet (2007) points out, however, less prominent in the
coverage over this case was the issue of the federal isolation
order itself, around which there were a number of legal

uncertainties that relate directly to the Siracusa Principles. Noting that the courts have historically tended to show deference to the expert advice of public health officials in such cases, Parmet identifies unanswered legal questions over issues including how long someone like Speaker can be held before a hearing of his case and whether other, less restrictive, control programmes should be in place before an isolation order is issued. The way the Speaker story ended was a salutary lesson in why attempts to clarify rights protections in such cases is important: later tests showed that he did not in fact have XDR-TB at all, but rather 'only' MDR-TB (a serious condition in itself, but one that can be treated – albeit not with first-line drugs).

The issues over Speaker were about the legal authority of public health officials to forcibly detain those infected with a transmissible disease, but in some cases the issues are more military than legal in character. To return to the West African Ebola example, the Liberian government's militarized approach to quarantine was heavily criticized on human rights grounds. This first came to international attention when the West Point district of the capital Monrovia was quarantined in August 2014. As part of the government's declared State of Emergency, the peninsula was cordoned off from the rest of the city, following unrest at an Ebola treatment centre. Armed police were stationed on the quarantine line to prevent residents of West Point crossing into the rest of Monrovia. Violence broke out: stones were thrown. In response, the police used tear gas and batons in an attempt to control the growing crowd. One boy attempting to escape West Point was shot dead; another two young men were wounded (MacDougall 2014). Much of the international media reporting of these incidents, unhelpfully, referred to West Point as 'notorious' and a 'slum', further stigmatizing a community that was already being blamed within Liberia for spreading Ebola (e.g. MacDougall 2014; Shute 2014). Nevertheless, the international attention these events attracted did help to put pressure on the government of Liberia to change course after eleven days of the planned twenty-one-day quarantine period, including pressure from the African Union, which called on its members to 'respect the principle of free movement, and to ensure that all restrictions are in line with recommendations from the relevant international organisations' (African Union 2014). As Zidar (2015: 513–14) notes, compulsory quarantine has a direct impact on the right to liberty, meaning that the Siracusa Principles again come into play.

In their research into the social consequences of forcible quarantine in Liberia during Ebola, Pellecchia et al. (2015) conducted interviews, focus groups and observations amongst the West Point community. They found, perhaps not surprisingly, anger about the actions of the authorities. Yet this anger, revealingly, was not just about the impact that the quarantine had upon residents' right to liberty (as well as related rights, such as the right to work, for those whose employment lay beyond the quarantine line), but also about the failure of the state to provide adequate health services for the West Point community. One respondent is reported as saying

> We didn't understand the logic ... Instead of helping us with clinics and ambulances they pushed us in. What were we supposed to do? Keep the dead inside? No-one came to educate us ... what is Ebola? They talked about a virus that came all in a sudden and the day after we witnessed the police with sticks and guns. (Pellecchia et al. 2015: 5)

The obvious justifications for the Liberian government's approach are the scale of the emergency the country faced, and the lack of obvious alternative forms of action – particularly given the country's limited resources for combatting the epidemic. Yet, in terms of the Siracusa Principles, we may certainly doubt both the effectiveness and the necessity of the Liberian government's actions. Zidar (2015: 514) argues that a medical justification for restricting liberty places an obligation on the government to provide 'adequate medical examination, care, and treatment.' This certainly seems not to have been provided in West Point.

Beyond this, not only could the forcible quarantine be seen as an unreasonable derogation of rights, it may even have been counter-productive, creating resistance rather than trust in the authorities and failing to deliver the kinds of behaviour change that experts saw as essential to reducing disease transmission. The political context of Liberia, a country still recovering from civil war in which trust in government was already low and where the arrival of troops rarely meant good news for local communities, was a particularly sensitive environment for such coercive 'top-down' quarantine measures (Pellecchia et al. 2015). Just as we saw with HIV-related travel restrictions, policies intended to deliver security at the expense of human rights and civil liberties can have unintended consequences that are detrimental to public health.

The Right to Health: Prevention, Treatment and Control

What if we were to reframe the debate, away from 'rights versus security' to viewing such policy dilemmas as being about balancing competing rights claims? Certainly it could be argued that, in any case of infectious disease, the wider community's right to health may be endangered by a contagious individual's decision to exercise their own right to liberty, and so on. Such conflicts of rights are common in a whole range of fields, not only in health. The Universal Declaration of Human Rights indeed allows for limitations to be placed on rights and freedoms in order to protect the rights and freedoms of others (Zidar 2015: 507). In a public health emergency, such conflicts of rights can be particularly acute.

Health itself is recognized as a human right. But although much has been written about the 'right to health' – and it has been enshrined in a range of international documents, including the WHO Constitution, the 1946 Universal Declaration on Human Rights, and the 1966 International Covenant on Economic, Social and Cultural Rights – there remains much debate over precisely what the right to health entails, what concomitant obligations it imposes, and how it should be balanced against competing rights.

Having a right to health cannot, of course, mean that we can expect never to suffer from disease or infirmity (the WHO Constitution talks about 'the enjoyment of the highest *attainable* standard of health' rather than setting a benchmark). The right to access medical care is perhaps the most obvious (and one of the most common) ways in which the right to health has been translated into concrete claims (see, for example, the discussion of access to antiretroviral medicines in chapter 2). But, according to the UN's Office of the High Commissioner for Human Rights (OHCHR 2008), the right to health in fact extends much further than this, including determinants of health such as access to clean water and adequate housing and, most importantly for our purposes, 'The right to prevention, treatment and control of diseases.' It is fundamental to the right to health that these rights are provided for without discrimination (in the words of the WHO Constitution, 'without distinction of race, religion, political belief, economic or social condition'). Under this broader vision of the right to health, it is not only during an emergency that the right comes into play, but also in whether (or not) effective action is taken to prevent an outbreak occurring in the first place. Here, the rights of individuals and collectivities are much more easily reconciled.

A number of factors can influence whether or not the right to prevention, treatment and control of diseases is realized in practice. Some diseases are more easily preventable than others, either because technological measures (such as vaccines) exist, or because of a disease's mode of transmission. Health system capacity is another key factor in effective disease control. The West African Ebola outbreak once again offers an example of the way in which health system weaknesses in diagnosis, surveillance and infection control can result in a failure to effectively prevent disease transmission through a population – even in the case of a virus which, in purely public health terms, is not especially difficult to contain. Human behaviour is another key factor, including how we as individuals and communities respond to an outbreak (do we heed public health advice, or not?) and the extent to which prevention methods are socially and culturally acceptable. HIV prevention efforts in many societies have faced these challenges, as some people have failed to change their behaviours (or have not been educated that change is necessary), or have found prevention methods such as condoms to be unacceptable for religious or cultural reasons. Vaccination campaigns – certainly the most effective form of disease prevention short of complete eradication – have also often been undermined by socio-cultural opposition, in both the Global North, where anti-vaccination movements flourish (Parker 2015), and in the Global South, where polio vaccinators in Pakistan, Afghanistan and northern Nigeria have faced intense opposition, and in some cases lethal violence (Ghinai et al. 2013; Peckham 2018). The provision of treatment is an area in which, in many ways, it is much more straightforward to determine whether or not the right to health is being realized. But again, there are a range of factors that can make that realization more or less possible in practice, including the availability and cost of treatments, the size of the demand, and the capacity of the health system to deliver it.

On the one hand, then, disease prevention, treatment and control is proclaimed as a human right, whilst on the other it is clearly a highly difficult task, with a variety of biological, social, economic and political determinants of success. Where does this leave the right to prevention, treatment and control of diseases? The Committee on Economic, Social and Cultural Rights' 'General Comment 14' was designed to elaborate on the International Covenant on Economic, Social and Cultural Rights' provisions on the right to health, specifically by detailing what obligations the covenant places on states in relation to realizing the right to health. General Comment 14's discussion of the right to prevention, treatment and control of diseases elaborates some of the things that all governments are required to do:

> 16. 'The prevention, treatment and control of epidemic, endemic, occupational and other diseases' (art. 12.2 (c)) requires the establishment of prevention and education programmes for behaviour-related health concerns such as sexually transmitted diseases, in particular HIV/AIDS, and those adversely affecting sexual and reproductive health, and the promotion of social determinants of good health, such as environmental safety, education, economic development and gender equity. The right to treatment includes the creation of a system of urgent medical care in cases of accidents, epidemics and similar health hazards, and the provision of disaster relief and humanitarian assistance in emergency situations. The control of diseases refers to States' individual and joint efforts to, inter alia, make available relevant technologies, using and improving epidemiological surveillance and data collection on a disaggregated basis, the implementation or enhancement of immunization programmes and other strategies of infectious disease control.

This does not, however, help us to understand how the rights of the infected and the uninfected can be reconciled during an outbreak. The catch-all phrase 'implementation or enhancement of immunization programmes and other strategies of infectious disease control' certainly puts an obligation on states to attempt to control outbreaks when they occur, but it does not solve the balance of rights question: at what point should individual rights be sacrificed for the wider community's right to be protected during an outbreak? The Siracusa Principles, as we have seen above, provide slightly more guidance in this regard, but even they do not provide an easy to apply resolution to the issue.

This is a political issue as much as it is a public health or a legal one. Ronald Bayer (2007: 1101) has written that public health gives rise to 'inherent tensions between the good of the collective and the individual' and argues that it is essential that we (or, perhaps more pertinently, our governments) 'are fully cognizant of difficult trade-offs when we make policy determinations.' As Birgit Toebes (2015) has argued, whilst the right to health might be able to strengthen claims for public health to be protected against other interests (e.g. trade interests), health security cases are difficult because they often pit the collective right to health against the individual's right to health.

In any case, governments around the world have not always been enthusiastic about the right to health and many refuse to recognize it within their own societies. As Cooper, Kirton and Schrecker (2007: 232) argued a decade ago, the 'claim that health is a human right ... still has little appeal beyond the human rights community.' That remains true today. Governments are much more likely to engage in a discourse of security than a discourse of rights when it comes to the threat of infectious diseases. Protecting the population in a 'war against the microbes' is generally viewed as a far more attractive political stance than trying to guarantee the public's right to prevention, treatment and control of disease, or an infected individual's rights to liberty, treatment and dignity. The reframing of the tensions in this area as a conflict of rights, therefore, has more ethical than policy appeal. For policymakers, the trade-off remains one between individual rights and national security.

Despite this book's enthusiastic defence of politics, politics can't always be relied on to solve such debates in ways that are either effective in public health terms, or normatively just. As we have seen throughout this chapter, a politics of fear, discrimination and repression often takes over once an emergency hits. In part this is generated by feelings of insecurity around disease that long pre-date its framing as a national security priority in the 1990s and 2000s. In evolutionary terms, such fear may, indeed, be an essential human survival mechanism. Yet, as Mika Aaltola (2012a) has argued, we also need to be aware of the ways in which contemporary policy responses to disease feed and sustain anxiety, and the power dynamics, at both the national and global levels, that generate fear – and frequently, as we have seen – generate policies and practices that are *both* injurious to rights *and* self-defeating.

Conclusion

Political debate over the appropriate balance between individual and collective rights – or between individual rights and public health security – does not only mean arguing about the rights and wrongs of particular policy interventions in particular cases. It also requires a broader set of political debates around power, justice and inequality, asking whose rights are being breached, and in the name of whose security? The right to health is not a strong claim in many places. And even civil and political rights, which have become more widely accepted, might not always 'win out' against security. Nevertheless, they can and have in some cases been important in protecting individuals from discriminatory treatment, or in securing access to vital resources such as medicines. Human rights provides an alternative language for talking about threats to individual and collective health, and for highlighting the further threats to individual rights and liberties that security-driven responses to public health crises can bring. The very existence of human rights concepts and human rights instruments such as the Siracusa Principles shows that another politics of health is possible – indeed already exists. This allows us to start building a picture of what an alternative 'pro-health politics' might look like.

The focus in this chapter has been on the balancing of rights with security. Viewing diseases as security threats can and does affect how this balance comes to be struck, whether the supposed threat comes from Haitian refugees or residents of a city's more deprived neighbourhoods. Sometimes this threat becomes associated with an individual carrier of disease – as with Mary Mallon, who we met at the beginning of this chapter. But often the threat is portrayed more widely than this, as coming from a particular section of the community, or a particular part of the globe that comes to be seen as a danger to others. Such divides can run along many fault lines: of nationality, race, sexuality, gender or social class. As is so often the case with human rights, the marginalized are far more likely than the privileged to have their rights traduced. Defending them requires a wider politics, one that is alert to the global and local inequalities that put certain groups at greater risk from disease, and that then portray those groups as threatening. In the next chapter I address this issue, examining the ways in which the securitization of disease further entrenches inequalities, protecting some at the expense of others and promoting a worldview that 'denigrates large regions of the world as dangerous – disease-ridden, poverty-stricken and disaster-prone' (Bankoff 2001: 29).

– 5 –

Global Inequalities and Differential Disease Risks

Few populations around the world have experienced the levels of insecurity that poor Haitians have faced in the twentieth and twenty-first centuries. After decades of authoritarian rule, armed conflict, economic stagnation and natural disaster, Haiti finds itself towards the bottom of the global league tables of human wellbeing. In the 2016 Human Development Index, it came joint 163rd out of 188 – by far the lowest ranking country in the Americas (UNDP 2016). Following the earthquake of 2010 that devastated much of the capital city Port au Prince and surrounding areas, that insecurity was compounded by a new threat: cholera, a disease that had not been seen in Haiti for 100 years.

The cruel irony of the Haiti cholera outbreak – which at the time of writing has seen over 800,000 people infected, and has caused over 9,500 deaths (PAHO/WHO 2017: 2) – was that the disease was introduced into the country by United Nations peacekeepers who were, in theory, there to help protect and support the population. Although the UN initially tried to deny responsibility, an independent investigation declared with some confidence that the source of the outbreak was the Mirebalais camp of MINUSTAH, the UN mission in Haiti. Specifically, failures in the camp's sanitation facilities had allowed faecal matter to leak into a tributary of the Arbonite river (Cravioto et al. 2011). The peacekeeping troops stationed at Mirebalais were from Nepal – another of the world's poorest countries, sitting just a few places above Haiti at 144th in the 2016 Human Development Index. Cholera is endemic in Nepal.

Arguments over the UN's moral and legal responsibilities to the victims of the Haiti cholera outbreak continue. But it is clear that the health insecurity faced by those who have contracted the disease is inextricably related to poverty and inequality. Once cholera had been brought into the country, poverty, the lack of sanitation and water infrastructure, and weaknesses in the health system made Haitians more vulnerable to contracting the disease, and more likely to die if they did. Had the outbreak occurred in a wealthier nation, it is certain that we would have seen nothing like the levels of sickness and death that Haiti has experienced. One important lesson here is that we live in a world of highly differentiated exposure to infectious disease risk, and wide disparities in the likelihood of receiving effective medical treatment if and when we do contract a disease.

In the previous chapter, I looked primarily at the ways in which security-based responses to disease can endanger individual rights and liberties given the propensity of governments to prioritize security in the context of a public health emergency. In this chapter, I build on that discussion to examine the ways in which the securitization of disease articulates with global inequalities. I make two arguments. First, I show that much of the discourse on 'global health security' fails to properly recognize inequalities in exposure to risk. Disease outbreaks, including outbreaks of 'Emerging and Re-emerging Infectious Diseases' (ERIDs), are generally presented in this discourse as an inevitable fact of life in the 'global village'; risks that are shared globally. In the oft-quoted words of the WHO's 2007 *World Health Report*, 'an outbreak or epidemic in any one part of the world is only a few hours away from becoming an imminent threat somewhere else' (WHO 2007: x). According to this logic, we exist in a global community of fate, in which the infectious diseases that affect some will ultimately affect us all, and in which all countries therefore have an equal stake in pursuing global health security.

This is an understandable discourse for the WHO to engage in, given that it wants to convince richer states to play a major role in global disease control efforts and to help poorer countries to improve their own ability to detect and contain emerging outbreaks early. However, I argue in the first part of this chapter that one downside of this global health security narrative is that it tends to 'flatten out' global inequalities, obscuring disparities in risk. I show that the root causes of outbreaks are at least as much about political economy as they are about microbiology. Global political and economic structures increase the risks that diseases will emerge in certain places, and increase the harm to populations in these places once they do. When a major transnational outbreak does occur, the resultant risks are not equally shared: and ironically, the countries most vocal in their concerns about the security implications of infectious diseases are those that are most insulated from their impacts.

In the second part of the chapter, I look at contemporary attempts to deliver global health security, showing that these are characterized by interlocking systems of disease surveillance and containment. In the third part, I build on this to argue that whilst these aims are important in themselves, they do little to address the political and economic inequalities that lie at the heart of the global infectious disease problem. Too often, global responses are in fact designed in ways that maintain rather than challenge existing inequalities. In other words, securitization has generated a modality of response that may indeed have reduced the overall risk of transnational disease outbreaks to some extent, but which has done so in ways that have unequal effects on the security of individuals and populations. Surveillance can help detect outbreaks more quickly, but does little to prevent them occurring in the first place. Meanwhile, the containment of disease outbreaks has been characterized by an emergency mode of operation in which concerted efforts are made to bring the threat under control, but once that has been achieved attention then quickly moves on, without addressing the structural inequalities that led to the outbreak occurring in the first place. It is true that new diseases will emerge (as they have always done) and that in some cases this will lead to outbreaks that are difficult to deal with. But at the same time, there are a variety of preventive steps that could limit these possibilities, which are not taken. One of the most important reasons why they are not taken is that doing so would require a level of resource transfer from the rich to the poor that is deemed unacceptable to the countries who talk so much about the threat diseases pose to their security – another demonstration of the fact that while the West says it wants security, it does not pursue it at all costs. This is a political choice, one that, if it is to be challenged, can only be challenged politically.

Inevitable and Shared Global Risks

In chapter 1, I discussed the ways in which Emerging Infectious Diseases (EIDs) came to be seen as one of the most pressing forms of global health security threat – a view that was promoted by medical and public health experts and adopted by key security policy communities, especially in the Global North. Concerns about cross-border transmission lay at the heart of the concern with EIDs, captured neatly in the title of the US National Intelligence Council's report, *The Global Infectious Disease Threat and Its Implications for the United States* (NIC 2000). The report's title is clear: the threat is global, and even rich countries such as the US can't avoid being exposed to the resultant risks. Whilst this is true – pathogens can and do travel globally – I focus in this section on two problematic assumptions that lie behind this discourse: that the threats are inevitable, and that all are equally vulnerable.

There is often a sense in political discussions of global-ization, around everything from financial markets to popular culture, that individual governments are powerless to resist its onward march, and that the best they can do is attempt to capture some of the upsides of life in a globalized world whilst trying to mitigate some of the negative impacts. Such a discourse of powerlessness, however, can obscure some of the underlying causes of globalization-related challenges. We can see this happening clearly in policy discussions around EIDs.

Although new diseases have emerged regularly through-out human history, and old diseases have evolved in ways that make them no longer susceptible to available medical treatments (seen most clearly in the growing challenge of antimicrobial resistance), it is highly problematic to divorce these biological processes from human actions (and gov-ernment policies). Indeed, the Institute of Medicine Report that played such an important role in bringing EIDs to the attention of security policymakers (Lederberg and Oaks 1992: chapter 2) set out a number of ways in which human action has been a factor in the emergence of new pathogens, or in their spread to previously unaffected populations. These include agricultural practices (as with Bovine spon-giform encephalopathy (BSE) and Japanese encephalitis), urbanization (Dengue, Lassa fever, Yellow fever), changing patterns of land usage leading to increased contact between humans and animal disease hosts (rabies), the long-distance transportation of animals (Rift Valley fever), intravenous drug use (Hepatitis C, HIV), and the deterioration of public health infrastructure (measles). All of these 'emerging infec-tion' threats have a direct link to human actions and, as the report notes (p. 42), 'Changes in the environment and in human behavior, as well as other factors, may increase the chances that dissemination will occur.' Scientific research since the 1992 report has provided even more evidence of the links between human actions and disease emergence and spread. Anthropogenic climate change has been a particular focus of attention, including the impact that rising global temperatures are having on the endemicity of mosquito-borne diseases (e.g. Patz et al. 1996), although this is only one of a much broader range of health impacts that will accrue as global temperatures rise (see Watts et al. 2015).

Once it is accepted that human actions, and social, political, economic and environmental policies, are significant factors in the causation of EIDs, the relationship of those diseases to insecurity begins to shift subtly. Rather than being inevitable exogenous threats to human life, these pathogens can be seen as – at least in part – products of local, national and international social, economic and political arrangements. The threat, in other words, is not simply 'nature in action'. Once that is recognized, it becomes clear that, at least implicitly, 'security' from disease is continually being traded off against other goals and interests, whether that be the economic gains to be made from deforestation, the higher costs of less intensive farming practices, or the difficulties of grappling with the complex social and economic causes of intravenous drug use. It is not possible to completely prevent disease emergence. But there are potential policy options that would significantly reduce the likelihood and impact of disease outbreaks. A lack of scientific evidence is not the stumbling block here: the problem of EIDs is exacerbated by (either implicit or explicit) political and economic choices.

Yet the discourses of risk and vulnerability that pervade much health security rhetoric pay scant attention to these choices, instead reaffirming an assumption of inevitability. The NIC's 2000 report on *The Global Infectious Disease Threat and its Implications for the United States* is a prime example. The report sets out three future scenarios for infectious disease threats, but argues that the most likely is 'Deterioration, Then Limited Improvement' in which

> In the next decade, under this scenario, negative demographic and social conditions in developing countries, such as continued urbanization and poor health care capacity, remain conducive to the spread of infectious diseases; persistent

poverty sustains the least developed countries as reservoirs of infection; and microbial resistance continues to increase faster than the pace of new drug and vaccine development. During the subsequent decade, more positive demographic changes such as reduced fertility and aging populations; gradual socioeconomic improvement in most countries; medical advances against childhood and vaccine-preventable killers such as diarrheal diseases, neonatal tetanus, and measles; expanded international surveillance and response systems; and improvements in national health care capacities take hold in all but the least developed countries.

Here we see a curious narrative of virtual inevitability. Although some progress might happen (as a result of 'reduced fertility', 'aging populations' and 'socio-economic improvements'), the benefits that this would bring in terms of reducing infectious disease threats are presented as a useful byproduct of other developments, not as something that is amenable to policy action. It is only in the medical and public health fields ('medical advances', 'improvements in national health care capacities') that deliberate positive interventions are foreseen. And whilst health can be improved, the report holds out little hope for this happening in the 'least developed countries.' Although presented as a public health assessment of the threat to the United States, beneath the surface of this report are some implicit ideological views about the role of governments (including foreign governments) in forwarding socio-economic change and addressing global poverty and inequality. Hidden here is the discourse of helplessness in the face of globalization.

If the discourse on the causes of disease emergence is implicitly ideological, so too are understandings of what that risk means for different societies around the world. McInnes and Roemer-Mahler (2017) show that understandings of global health risk are socially constructed, as are understandings of global health security, and that changes in perceptions of infectious diseases in recent years are part of bigger changes in societal understandings of risk. As they argue, 'The sense of vulnerability to health risks, especially disease outbreaks, cannot be separated from the broader feeling of social vulnerability, evident not only in public policy but also in cultural products' (McInnes and Roemer-Mahler 2017: 1315). The social context within which new perceived disease threats emerge therefore plays an important role in whether diseases in general, and specific diseases in particular, come to be seen as security threats (whether national, regional or global). The wider security environment plays a role in this. And so does our imagination of the world beyond our borders, and our own place within that world.

In chapter 3, we saw the ways in which reinvigorated fears about the threat posed by biological weapons emerged in the aftermath of the attacks of 11 September 2001. Both terrorist groups and 'rogue' individuals came to be seen as potential sources of biological threat. The idea that pathogens are a national security issue was already becoming embedded within the security policies of many countries (especially in the Global North) by that stage, but 9/11 and the 'War on Terror' added a new urgency to this health security narrative (Aaltola 2012b: 65). Thus, pathogens became integrated into wider societal fears and insecurities.

Scientific as well as political developments can affect societal views of risk. The shift to what Stefan Elbe (2018) has called the 'molecular view of life' has also played a role in these growing feelings of insecurity. We now know more than ever before about pathogens. We can genetically sequence viruses and track the mutations that occur. We can speculate about potential future mutations and what they might mean in terms of the epidemiology of future outbreaks. As Elbe (2018: 234) rightly points out, without this molecular knowledge 'we would not even know about the smoldering cocktail of biological danger that lurks just beyond the limits of what we can perceive with the naked eye.'

The limits of what we perceive are in part about scale and our inability to view the molecular level without sophisticated scientific equipment. Yet our geographical horizons, and imaginations, matter too in conditioning how we think about pathogenic risks. Claims about the dangers posed by other, generally poorer, parts of the globe underlie many of the current anxieties, of public and policymakers alike. We saw this clearly in the cases of Ebola in West Africa, SARS, and even HIV, where threats from diseased populations 'over there' were seen as a security problem for Western nations. Here, global political and economic inequalities and science-based understandings of disease risk come together in interesting and powerful combinations. The world is conceptualized in much of the global health security discourse as a single community of fate, but with a strong (although often unstated) belief that the source of risk to that community emanates mainly from the global poor. The involvement of the rich in creating the global inequalities and in driving the political and economic processes that exacerbate disease emergence are rarely if ever acknowledged in policy documents and statements. We are not so far away as we might like to think from the orientalist tropes about primitive and unhygienic societies that characterized nineteenth-century 'tropical medicine' in Africa and Asia. Such orientalist ideas are rarely so explicitly stated in contemporary political discourse on disease, but they are often not far below the surface. One person who did come close to explicitly making such a case was Robert Kaplan in his (in)famous examination of West Africa, 'The coming anarchy', in which he wrote of the region

> becoming the symbol of worldwide demographic, environmental, and societal stress, in which criminal anarchy emerges as the real 'strategic' danger. Disease, overpopulation, unprovoked crime, scarcity of resources, refugee migrations, the increasing erosion of nation-states and international borders, and the empowerment of private armies, security firms, and international drug cartels are now most tellingly demonstrated through a West African prism. West Africa provides an appropriate introduction to the issues, often extremely unpleasant to discuss, that will soon confront our civilization. (Kaplan 1994: 46)

Kaplan's analysis was widely critiqued, and in African Studies has become a notorious example of the caricaturing of (West) Africa by neorealist scholars in the immediate post-Cold War era (e.g. Dalby 1998; Dunn 2004). But despite its many flaws, Kaplan's piece both reflected and bolstered a wider imaginary of West Africa as an endlessly troubled region of conflict and chaos that is explicitly contrasted with 'our civilization', in the process writing out of the narrative any blame on richer countries for creating the 'anarchy' that he claimed to find there. The fact that the image was a gross simplification of lived realities in West Africa did little to reduce the power of the narrative, and disease came to be incorporated as part of the 'failed state thesis' (especially, as we saw in chapter 2, in the case of AIDS).

Although not as bleak as Kaplan's analysis – and always framed in a way which seemed supportive of rather than dismissive of the national governments in the three most affected countries – this narrative of West Africa's inherent instability was present in some of the most high-profile speeches made during the 2014–16 Ebola outbreak, in which WHO Director-General Margaret Chan told the UN Security Council that 'an exponentially rising caseload threatens to push governments to the brink of state failure' (Chan 2014) and Barack Obama used a press conference at the CDC in Atlanta to tell the world that 'this is an epidemic that is not just a threat to regional security – it's a potential threat to global security if these countries break down, if their economies break down, if people panic. That has profound effects on all of us, even if we are not directly contracting the disease' (Obama 2014b).

Here the weakness of West African states, a weakness that allowed the Ebola outbreak to escalate out of control, is firmly framed as posing a threat to the rest of the world – and imposing burdens on the Western governments who will be required to intervene to deal with the fall-out. More progressive readings of the Ebola case were no less rooted in claims about the weakness of West African states, and particularly their health systems. All of the lessons learned reports (rightly) pointed to the critical weaknesses of those health systems as a significant factor in allowing what could have been a small and contained outbreak to become a major regional crisis. Less often was there a recognition of the historical processes that produced those weaknesses. Such arguments were largely confined to the academic community (e.g. Anderson and Beresford 2016).

All of this helps illustrate securitization's power, in which socially constructed ideas about risk generate a worldview according to which emerging disease threats have to be continually monitored and stopped in their tracks before they get the chance to spread too far. People, animals, food and other goods are constantly moving back and forth across borders. An infected individual can move between almost any two points on the globe in a matter of hours. The result, in the words of the UK's *Health is Global* strategy is that 'Poor health is more than a threat to any one country's economic and political viability – it is a threat to the economic and political interests of all countries' (HM Government 2008: 14). The WHO concurs, arguing that 'the public health security of all countries depends on the capacity of each to act effectively and contribute to the security of all' (WHO 2007: xiii).

Despite the narrative that globalization has created a world of shared risks, there is a clear sense that in reality some (in the Global North) are threatened by others (in the Global South). Disease threats are more likely to emerge in poorer countries as a result of poverty and other social and economic issues, and containing them there helps avoid richer countries being exposed to the threat, Yet, as I go on to argue in the final section of this chapter, contemporary approaches to strengthening 'global health security' do little to engage with the structural inequalities that produce this situation, instead focusing on surveillance and outbreak containment in ways that bear out the argument that framing diseases as security threats tends to generate short-term emergency responses, rather than the longer-term engagements that would actually be required to reduce inequalities and address the different risks faced by different populations.

Delivering Global Health Security: Surveillance and Containment

As we have already seen, one of the key insights of securitization theory (e.g. Buzan, Waever and de Wilde 1998) is that successfully securitizing an issue can legitimate an exceptional emergency response, allowing the authorities to take actions that wouldn't be possible in 'normal' situations. As we saw in the previous chapter, national governments and local authorities facing an outbreak have often given themselves the power to institute emergency arrangements that would otherwise be considered breaches of civil liberties, human rights and due process. These have included many different types of measures, such as forcible isolation and quarantine and strict border controls. In addition, governments have often introduced measures aimed at 'social distancing' during outbreaks, such as closing schools (as Mexico did during H1N1 'swine flu') or introducing curfews (as the government of Sierra Leone did during Ebola). Typically, these emergency powers are exercised for a limited time only, with things returning to normal once the outbreak has been brought under control.

In between outbreak crises, the concept of 'preparedness' (Nelson et al. 2007) has increasingly entered the security policy lexicon, partly in response to infectious disease threats but also in response to other challenges, including natural disasters and climate change. The aim of public health preparedness is generally seen as being to help prevent, mitigate and recover from a health emergency, and includes such diverse investments as developing the laboratory capacities to promptly detect and diagnose outbreaks; improving the ability of the public health infrastructure to deal with a public health emergency; ensuring that different levels and departments of government share information and coordinate their responses; and putting in place plans and systems to enable the different emergency services to work together. Ongoing efforts such as routine vaccination programmes are also seen as having an important part to play in improving the resilience of society in the face of a major outbreak.

In this section, however, my main interest is in the cooperative initiatives that have been put in place at the global level following a series of high-profile international outbreak events in the early twenty-first century. These efforts fall into the same two categories as the domestic measures discussed above: emergency response during a disease emergency, and preparedness activities in between times. My argument here, however, is that these activities do not significantly challenge the global inequalities that give rise to increased levels of disease risk. Rather, the emphasis has been on surveillance in between crises, and containment during them: a 'whack-a-mole' approach to infectious diseases that does little to address the underlying sources of vulnerability. Inevitably this leads to the suspicion that these 'global health security' efforts are more concerned with the security of some than others, and that the key driver behind these global efforts is the desire to protect the rich, developed world from the 'dangerous' global poor (Rushton 2011).

Andrew Lakoff (2010) has pointed to the fact that surveillance is at the heart of the 'global health security' regime. In recent years there have been a number of initiatives – both technical and political – designed to ensure that outbreaks of diseases that have potential cross-border implications are identified early, and that the resulting information is communicated rapidly between governments around the world. Such efforts are not entirely new: two of the first accomplishments of the WHO were the establishment of the Global Influenza Surveillance Network in 1947 and the adoption of the International Sanitary Regulations in 1951 – after a century of failed attempts to devise a system of worldwide disease surveillance (Fidler 2001). Those regulations (later revised and renamed the International Health Regulations, and discussed in chapter 1) required governments to inform the WHO of cases of those diseases then seen as posing an international threat, and to put in place measures at ports and airports to prevent their spread across borders (WHA 1951). However, the only 'notifiable diseases' were plague, cholera, yellow fever, smallpox, typhus and relapsing fever. Concerted attempts to develop a truly global 'early warning system' that covered all infectious diseases of international concern are comparatively recent. As Lakoff argues, those efforts are closely associated with the coming to the fore of 'emerging infectious diseases' and a recognition of the need to develop surveillance capacities not only for 'known' pathogenic threats such as influenza, but also for outbreaks of new diseases.

The WHO's Global Outbreak Alert and Response Network (GOARN) began its work in the late 1990s and was the foremost multilateral effort to improve global disease surveillance capacities. SARS in 2003 was its first major test (Heymann and Rodier 2004). In purely surveillance terms, GOARN performed relatively well, identifying the emerging issue in China even before the national authorities, who initially reported the outbreak as being influenza. As we saw in chapter 1, the problems the WHO faced were on the political more than the technical side, with China initially seeking to cover up what was happening – an early indication of some of the consequences of the WHO's move away from the traditional reliance on national disease reporting structures (under which the WHO only came to learn about outbreaks from national ministries of health), to a truly global information network, that 'undermined national governments' traditional control of public health knowledge, making a global form of disease surveillance possible' (Lakoff 2010: 72). Although GOARN, which boasts over 600 partners worldwide (WHO 2015), is now well established as a key part of the global disease surveillance architecture, there are a number of other players operating in this space too, including national surveillance efforts; the US in particular maintains its own global surveillance capacities through both the Centers for Disease Control and Prevention (CDC n.d.) and the Department of Defense (Canas et al. 2000).

As information technology has advanced, disease surveillance has increasingly begun to shift online, with internet-based systems seeking out signs of unusual clusters of cases in order to be able to identify and locate emerging outbreaks – according to their proponents, doing so faster than national public health systems can manage. The techniques used by these different surveillance providers (some of which are private organizations, some of which are public–private partnerships) vary. Some, such as ProMED-mail (www.promedmail.org), rely on human reporting, usually by health professionals, to an online platform. Others seek to use automated algorithms to scour global news sources for evidence of unusual disease clusters. Although none of these systems is infallible, and big challenges remain in separating 'signal from noise' and minimizing false positives, in theory they offer the promise of better, faster and less politicized global disease surveillance – although, as Sara Davies (2014) has argued, such systems do not (at least currently) entirely circumvent the problem of state secrecy, especially in authoritarian regimes where information flows are tightly controlled.

Having identified an outbreak, hopefully early on, the next task the global health security regime has is to assess its severity and implications, and to disseminate that information to other countries and agencies that might need to take action. The IHR are supposed to provide the institutional framework for this information sharing – regardless of whether the outbreak in question is naturally occurring or manmade. Under the IHR, governments are required to report an outbreak with potential international consequences to the WHO within 24 hours. A WHO expert committee has the power to declare such an event a 'Public Health Emergency of International Concern' (PHEIC), and to make recommendations to other states on the measures they need to put in place. In principle this is a technocratic, science-based process. In practice, as we have seen in all of the major PHEICs since the revised IHR came into force in 2007, its application is highly political – and quickly becomes highly politicized.

If surveillance is the leitmotif of international global health security efforts between outbreaks, containment can be said to characterize current global responses once an emerging threat is identified. The 2005 revision of the IHR, indeed, brought a deliberate and marked shift towards containment, moving away from the previous attempts to tackle incoming disease threats at the border towards a much greater emphasis on containing outbreaks at source (Andrus et al. 2010). As with surveillance, the IHR includes core capacity requirements for containment, with countries expected to have (or to develop) the public health infrastructure to be able to mount an effective domestic response to prevent emerging outbreaks from developing into transnational pandemics. Where they have not been able to succeed in containing an outbreak, the international community has, in some cases, shown a willingness to intervene, as it did (albeit belatedly) with Ebola in Guinea, Liberia and Sierra Leone.

One of the challenges that has emerged in this area is the capacity of the international community to mount a response. It can be difficult to rapidly mobilize the funding, manpower and equipment required to address a major public health emergency – even when the political will to do so is there. If the need to improve surveillance was the policy priority in the aftermath of SARS, post-Ebola much of the policy discussion has been on improving global rapid-response capabilities in order to improve containment. The WHO has launched a Contingency Fund for Emergencies, designed to allow the organization to respond rapidly to public health emergencies and other humanitarian disasters. The target, set by the WHA in 2015, was for a fund of US$100 million (WHA 2015). At the time of writing in mid-2018, contributions to the fund stood at just under $70 million, with almost $14 million already having been allocated to address public health crises (WHO 2018a). The World Bank, meanwhile, established its own Pandemic Emergency Financing Facility, which made its first disbursements during the 2018 Ebola outbreak in the Democratic Republic of Congo (Evans 2018).

Surveillance and containment naturally go together under the new global health security regime: effective surveillance allows for the early detection of threats, which in turn makes containment at source possible. If a threat is detected too late, containment can't be an effective means of limiting cross-border spread. Both are heavily steeped in security logics, and indeed bear significant similarities in both approach and language (particularly when surveillance is termed, as it often is, 'epidemic intelligence'), to activities in other security fields.

Addressing Inequalities for Global Health Security?

Surveillance and rapid response capabilities are, of course, extremely important and can deliver significant health benefits. They might well, indeed, be considered prime examples of 'global public goods for health' (Commission on Macroeconomics and Health 2002). On their own terms, they are difficult to criticize. The problem, however, is less with what the global health security regime *is*, as with what it is *not*. As we will see in the next chapter, one key question is around which diseases are deemed worthy of such surveillance and response efforts, and the extent to which this reflects public health challenges around the world on the one hand, or national security agendas on the other. In this section, I continue my argument that a second issue is around its neglect of underlying causes of infectious disease outbreaks; the structural inequalities that were discussed in the first section of this chapter.

Jim Yong Kim, President of the World Bank, has noted that 'For too long, we have allowed a cycle of panic and neglect when it comes to pandemics: we ramp up efforts when there's a serious threat, then quickly forget about them when the threat subsides' (World Bank 2018). There is a strong recognition amongst global health experts and agencies that well-functioning national public health systems are a fundamental part of the solution to delivering global health security. As the *World Health Report* in 2007 put it,

> The first steps that must be taken towards global public health security, therefore, are to develop core detection and response capacities in all countries, and to maintain new levels of cooperation between countries to reduce the risks to public health security outlined above. This entails countries strengthening their health systems and ensuring they have the capacity to prevent and control epidemics that can quickly spread across borders and even across continents. Where countries are unable to achieve prevention and control by themselves, it means providing rapid, expert international disease surveillance and response networks to assist them – and making sure these mesh together into an efficient safety net (2005). (WHO 2007: xi)

The West African Ebola outbreak provided another opportunity for (re-)learning this lesson. The chronic weakness of the health systems in Guinea, Liberia and Sierra Leone was universally identified as a major factor in the failure to quickly identify and later contain the outbreak. It was only after concerted international efforts began in the latter part of 2014 that the epidemic finally began to be brought under control. The question, however, is whether the determined and holistic strengthening of health systems that is required is actually being done in practice – and if so, whether that is having wider impacts on addressing the global inequalities which, as was argued above, lie at the heart of health insecurity, or whether it is only being done in a way that treats the 'symptoms' of these inequalities – disease outbreaks of international security concern.

The above quote from the 2007 *World Health Report* is instructive here. It does not call for the holistic strengthening of health systems to equip them to deal with the full range of health challenges a country faces, but rather to ensure 'they have the capacity to prevent and control epidemics.' Where countries are 'unable to achieve prevention and control by themselves', it calls not for international aid to help them build a stronger health system, but instead for something much more specific: 'rapid, expert international disease surveillance and response networks to assist them.' The aim of these investments is equally explicit: not to improve health generally, still less to tackle socio-economic inequalities, but to make sure these systems 'mesh together into an efficient safety net'.

Some have argued that interventions and investments in surveillance and containment designed to strengthen global health security bring knock-on benefits for health systems' ability to deal with a much wider range of health problems. Rodier and colleagues (some of the key architects of the IHR revision process) have perhaps made this argument most strongly, claiming that such investments 'will strengthen not only global public health security but also the infra-structure needed to help broaden access to healthcare services and improve individual health outcomes, which would help break the cycles of poverty and political instability and thus contribute to national economic development and achievement of the Millennium Development Goals' (Rodier et al. 2007: 1448).

Politically, it may well be the case that the security 'sell' is an effective way of persuading rich countries to invest in developing the health systems of their poorer peers (Jain and Alam 2017; Kamradt-Scott 2015), particularly in an era where (arguably) more altruistic international aid spending seems to be coming under increasing pressure. Here, global health security (which interests wealthy countries) is a potential lever for achieving broader health goals – including addressing the massive global inequalities in health and healthcare. Ooms and colleagues (2017) are cautious optimists about this approach, arguing that this positive outcome is possible given careful programme design, although noting that it is not inevitable. Indeed, they explicitly draw a parallel with 'vertical' AIDS programmes which had the potential to have broader benefits for health systems, but often failed to deliver these in practice.

The win–win scenario is the ideal. There are, however, reasons to at least be curious about the extent to which we have seen these benefits accrue in the decade since the new IHR came into force. As noted above, the IHR set out a series of 'core capacities' that states must put in place in order to be able to comply with their surveillance, reporting and containment obligations. These include indicators on things including legislation, surveillance mechanisms and infrastructure, infection control capabilities, and so on (WHO 2013). At the time the IHR revisions were negotiated, it was recognized that poorer countries would need international support to develop these capacities. By 2015, it was clear that progress was slow, to say the least (Davies, Kamradt-Scott and Rushton, 2015: chapter 5). At the time of writing, the most recent WHO data (WHO 2017) still paints a sobering picture. In the 2017 implementation monitoring process, 41.75% of countries claimed to meet between 75 and 100% of the core capacity requirements, averaged across thirteen core capacity areas. A number of the world's poorest countries,[13] meanwhile, reported their implementation status at 40% or below, a decade after these capacities were supposed to be in place. If progress has been so limited on helping some of the poorest countries in the world to develop the core capacities that have been so widely seen as central to global health security, what is the likelihood that the broader investment that may produce the 'spin off' benefits of overall health system improvement has occurred?

It is instructive to look at the types of activities that *have* taken place where international assistance efforts have been pursued in the name of global health security. The (US-led) Global Health Security Agenda is a case in point. It has developed a series of eleven 'Action Packages', arranged around the prevention, detection and response to pathogenic threats (GHSA 2014). Whilst these do include measures on prevention, they are mainly targeted towards specific interventions seen to be of security relevance (e.g. around Antimicrobial Resistance (Prevent 1), Zoonotic Disease (Prevent 2), and Biosafety and Biosecurity (Prevent 3)). The exception is Prevent 4, on immunization, which seeks to achieve 'Effective protection through achievement and maintenance of immunization against measles and other epidemic-prone vaccine-preventable diseases.' Even to the extent that investments are being made in global health security, these remain located at the level of the health system. There is little or no discussion in global health security policy debates around the wider structural factors, not least socio-economic inequalities, that perpetuate infectious disease risks and contribute to insecurity.

The cycle of panic and neglect identified by Jim Yong Kim in the quote above has tended to characterize emergency response efforts, and does little to challenge this neglect (see also Price-Smith and Porreca 2016). The international response to Ebola in West Africa came late, but came eventually. Once the dust settled on the emergency, it became clear that the impact on the health systems of the three most affected countries had been severe. Not only had many health workers lost their lives (Evans, Goldstein and Popova 2015), but the diversion of resources to Ebola had caused mortality from other diseases, including malaria, HIV and tuberculosis, to increase. This led to calls for the wholesale rebuilding of these health systems, with increased resilience in order to be able to better withstand such shocks in future (e.g. Kieny and Dovlo 2015). But international commitment to this longer-term effort was limited. Attention quickly shifted to Latin America and the outbreak of Zika virus in that region. And it was not only the attention that shifted, but also the resources: $500 million of US funding for Ebola which had not been used at the end of the outbreak was diverted to Zika, owing to the refusal of Congress to authorize new emergency funding for Zika (Armour 2016). A study of the post-Ebola recovery by

Wagenaar and colleagues (2018) found that in the case of Liberia, primary healthcare indicators did eventually return to pre-Ebola levels, but they identified a continuing urgent need for health system strengthening efforts to build 'primary healthcare systems capable of mitigating collateral effects of the next emerging epidemic.'

It is often said that securitization leads to short-term emergency-focused responses. This seems to be borne out by the experience of Guinea, Liberia and Sierra-Leone post-Ebola, but it was also evidenced in some of the political discourse at the time of the outbreak. A quote from Barack Obama's speech about Ebola at the UN Security Council illustrates how underlying structural issues so often get left out of the disease and security discourse (and, consequently, left out of policy). In calling for greater global action, Obama recalled that 'One health worker in Sierra Leone compared fighting this outbreak to "fighting a forest fire with spray bottles".' He promised that 'With our help, they can put out the blaze' (Obama 2014a). The metaphor of 'putting out the blaze' of the Ebola outbreak is strongly redolent of notions of emergency response; of a short-term effort to bring an immediate crisis under control. The outbreak is portrayed as a natural disaster, like a flood or a forest fire, in which the international community helps with the immediate emergency, and then withdraws once the crisis has passed. Hidden within this view of the Ebola outbreak is the narrative of inevitability that we saw in the first section of this chapter: an event that could not have been foreseen – still less prevented.

Paul Farmer has argued that Ebola can better be seen as a *man-made* catastrophe rather than a natural one (Achenbach 2014). The structural inequalities that characterize the global political economy lay behind the Ebola outbreak, producing the widespread poverty, urban overcrowding, lack of trust in the authorities, under-resourced health systems, shortages of health workers and equipment, and much more that were the facilitating conditions for a single infection to become a large-scale health and humanitarian crisis. All of these problems could have been, and were, known before the first case of Ebola. The international community did (eventually) help put out the fire. But there has been little long-term positive legacy for the affected countries.

Recognizing that the scale of the Ebola outbreak was a result of inequalities in the global political economy would entail a much wider understanding of the ways in which 'health is global' – one that focuses not only on disease transmission as a global problem or as a global responsibility, but that also genuinely understands the extent to which the determinants of health are rooted in global inequalities. The absence of such considerations from the global health security policy discourse has had the effect of closing off more transformative solutions and reproducing a 'firefighting' mode of operation.

Conclusion

It would be too simplistic to blame the Global North for all of the world's health problems. Governments in the Global South must take their share of the blame too – especially those who (for reasons of poor governance, unwillingness, corruption or some other cause) have chosen not to invest in health care and have failed to take effective action on tackling domestic poverty and inequality. These governments have made political choices too – choices that can have severe implications for the health of their own citizens and populations beyond their borders. We will return to this in the next chapter. Here, though, the focus has been on the ways in which global socio-economic inequalities produce and exacerbate disease risks and the failure of current global responses to engage with that fact.

William Powers (cited in Guernica 2006) quotes a Bolivian tribal chief as saying 'Either share your wealth with us, or we'll share our poverty with you.' No doubt, addressing the inequalities discussed in this chapter would be a huge and costly endeavour. It might be seen as utopian to even think about it – beyond the bounds of political possibility. Even if that is true, however, it tells us something important: that despite all the rhetoric about diseases representing a major threat to national security, we are not seeing governments pursue that security at all costs. There continues to be a reluctance to invest to the extent required even to globally deliver the basic surveillance and containment capacities that are needed to improve responses to infectious disease outbreaks of international concern. Establishing the idea that real global health security requires far more than this – that it means a massive effort to address the structural inequalities that create and exacerbate insecurity – seems as far away as ever. Instead, in the discourse around emerging infectious disease risks, we see the coming together of two powerful narratives: that societies (especially Western societies) are in a state of constant vulnerability to external disease threats; and that there is little that can be done to reduce the scale of those threats. All we can do is try to insulate ourselves from their worst effects.

Behind this, of course, are political choices: choices that are, implicitly at least, answers to the questions of 'How much security do we need?' and 'What are we prepared to sacrifice in order to get it?'. There is a certain level of international willingness to devote resources to tackling *some* disease emergencies when they occur – at least once the West sees itself as being imperilled. But there is little evidence of an appetite for a longer-term (and larger) investment in reducing the sources of infectious disease risk. What we see in practice is what I called in this chapter the 'whack-a-mole' approach to dealing with health security threats as they arise.

AIDS, discussed in chapter 2, seems to be a welcome exception here. In the AIDS case, we *have* seen a much longer-term and more institutionalized response, both at the national and international levels. That response has sought to prevent new infections as well as to increase the number of PLWHA able to access treatment. In part, this is due to AIDS being a 'long-wave' event (Barnett 2006), unlike the shorter-lived but rapidly developing outbreaks that have been the focus of this chapter. Yet, as I argued in chapter 2, this long-term investment may not be entirely down to securitization, but also the linking of AIDS with other values, including the international development agenda. For sure, international AIDS programmes have created their own problems for national health systems. But they do at least offer an example, however imperfect, of a sustained international effort to address a disease crisis, but also to address some of the root causes of that crisis. A purely security framing of pandemic emergencies seems not to deliver the same results. This is another important element of what an alternative 'pro-health politics' might look like.

Having critiqued the ways in which the international community has responded to infectious disease outbreaks in this chapter, in the next I move on to look at health crises that have barely seen any response at all, examining the ways in which securitization has driven a particular form of prioritization within global health – one that again raises big questions about whose security really matters, and what they feel they need to be secured from.

– 6 –

Everyday Insecurities, Health Priorities and Global Agendas

In August 2016, *The Guardian* published a report from a maternity unit in the Kankan region of north-eastern Guinea (Maclean 2016). The country had been declared Ebola free two months previously. But while that major threat to the population's health was (finally, and for now) over, everyday health insecurities continued – indeed had been worsened by Ebola, which had claimed the lives of many of the country's health workers.

A baby was born, took one breath, then left the world again. No amount of the midwife pumping his legs up to his ribcage and back, or poking a finger hard and fast at his chest, would bring him back.

His 17-year-old mother lay in pain on the delivery table as her son was wrapped up in a yellow cloth. There was no time even for her to hold him, as another woman was about to give birth. The midwives quickly changed their bloodied robes and gloves. Because there was no other table, the second woman gave birth lying on the floor.

This time, the baby yelled as soon as she came out. She was healthy. While the midwives moved on to the next urgent case, their small delivery room filling up, she spent her first few minutes screaming on the concrete slab.

Welcome to life in Guinea, baby Katherine.

The UN Security Council convened to discuss Ebola, but not the fact that more than one in ten children in Guinea die before their fifth birthday, nor that Guinea has one of the highest maternal mortality rates in the world, with 679 women dying for every 100,000 births (UNICEF 2018). These losses of life are not considered to be an international security problem. Neither are they deemed a 'Public Health Emergency of International Concern' by the WHO. The daily grind of life and death, of family tragedies and personal pain, is treated in a way that is categorically different to the big global disease 'events'. This would not surprise a securitization theorist. Indeed, it seems to prove their point: things that come to be interpreted as security threats are those things that can be presented as an 'existential threat' to the state. If successfully securitized, they are given a degree of prioritization that doesn't normally get bestowed on 'merely political' issues.

In the previous chapter, I argued that global socio-economic inequalities are ignored at our peril, because they lie behind many of the infectious disease risks that so preoccupy security policymakers. Attempting to detect and contain outbreaks without tackling these underlying inequalities addresses the symptoms whilst ignoring the causes. Here, I push this argument further in arguing that mainstream security policy's limited vision of insecurity is distorting the global agenda in ways that privilege the health (or, more accurately the fears) of some over others. The resulting security-driven prioritizations create opportunity costs elsewhere, further entrenching inequalities. We can see this play out at both the national and international levels.

In this chapter, I explore how security concerns about disease captured in the concept of health security relate to broader health agendas. In the first section, using the example of medicine stockpiling, I show that securitization creates opportunity costs, as money that is spent on preparing for potential future threats cannot also be spent on other things, even if the utility of those preparedness activities is uncertain. Second, building on the discussion in chapter 5, I argue that the focus on rapidly spreading infectious disease outbreaks, whether man-made or naturally occurring, provides a very limited vision of global health insecurity and ignores the everyday health insecurities experienced by populations around the world. This needs to be understood as a political choice. Third, I show that other forms of global health politics do exist and can be capable of generating attention and resources. Returning to the ways in which health has been approached as an international development issue through processes such as the MDGs and the SDGs, I show that security is not the only game in town. In the final part of the chapter, I argue that the way in which securitization has impacted on the global health agenda is more fundamental than merely affecting whether one health issue or another is prioritized for investment. Securitization has also profoundly affected what we understand by 'global health'. It is not only prioritization that is political: de-prioritization is too.

Preparedness and Opportunity Costs: The Case of Stockpiling

One of the areas in which the trade-offs between disease threats that are seen as 'security relevant' and other health issues is most readily apparent is in spending decisions at the national level around pandemic preparedness. The creation of national strategic stockpiles of medicines and other supplies is an excellent example. Stockpiling has been carried out by some Western governments seeking to ensure that they have the medicines, vaccines and other resources available to be deployed in case of a major health emergency. The largest is the US Strategic National Stockpile (SNS), originally created under the Clinton Administration in 1999 amidst growing concerns about potential bioterrorist attacks. The SNS contains antibiotics, chemical antidotes, antitoxins, vaccines, antiviral drugs, personal protective equipment, ventilators and other medical supplies (CDC 2018). Warehoused at six or more classified locations (Sun 2018), according to the CDC, the cost of the medicines and supplies included in the SNS in 2018 stood at US$7 billion (CDC 2018).

Given its substantial cost, and in the light of the debates that we saw around the value for money of biodefence research in chapter 3, it is perhaps surprising that the SNS has not been more controversial than it has. Where discussions over the SNS have arisen, they have mostly been around how it should be managed and precisely what should be stockpiled, rather than over whether the resources could be better used elsewhere. One recent controversy has centred around the Trump Administration's plan to shift responsibility for the stockpile from the CDC to the Department of Health and Human Services. And although it was ostensibly created to address both bioterrorist attacks and naturally occurring outbreaks, some have argued that the SNS is disproportionately oriented towards the former rather than the latter. Georges Benjamin, Executive Director of the American Public Health Association, has said that the SNS should contain 'the stuff we need for the disasters we know we're going to have – like gloves, syringes, Cipro, penicillin, antibiotics, and influenza vaccines – versus the newest, sexiest version of the anthrax vaccine' (quoted in Sun 2018). In the UK, there has also been some debate around stockpiling, again focused on what is being warehoused. The most high-profile dispute has been over Tamiflu, an antiviral drug used to treat influenza (Elbe 2018; Jefferson et al. 2014; van Noorden 2014), where there have been questions asked about the UK government's decision in the 2000s to invest in huge quantities of a drug for which there was mixed evidence in terms of efficacy in case of a future pandemic, and also concerns around the commercial interests that some suspected lay behind this resource-intensive flu preparedness strategy (Cohen and Carter 2010). But even here the debate has focused on the specifics of what is stockpiled, not on the question of whether the resources could be better used to address other health problems.

The lack of a wider debate about the opportunity costs of stockpiling as a preparedness strategy for outbreak emergencies seems to suggest that the principle is generally accepted. Certainly there is a logical security case for doing it. In the event of a major public health emergency, no government (certainly no democratic government that had to face the public in a future election) would want to be in the position of not having, and not being able to get access to, the medications and equipment necessary to protect and treat their population. In the context of huge budgetary challenges facing health systems across the developed world (not to mention the developing world, to which we will shortly turn), however, this spending needs to be seen as a political choice rather than a technocratic public health decision. Even in the wealthiest countries, arguments over the affordability and rationing of drugs for cancer and myriad other conditions are ongoing. Why should drugs intended to treat certain types of potential future public health emergencies not be subject to the same types of debate over value for money and opportunity costs? The securitization theory answer is that this is what securitization does: it enables the breaking free from the financial restrictions that would otherwise apply – even though (given that pharmaceuticals have a shelf life, and the likelihood, timing and nature of future bioterrorist attacks or naturally occurring pandemics is in any case unknown) there is a real possibility that the drugs stockpiled in the name of preparedness may never actually be used.

The point here is not to judge whether the decision to stockpile medicines against a future public health emergency is right or wrong – future events will determine that as much as anything else – but rather to make it clear that doing so is the result of conscious political decisions. Recognizing that allows us to at least open up political questions around prioritization that security discourses frequently obscure.

As well as recognizing stockpiling as a (contestable) political choice, we also need to be alive to the wider international political effects of such a policy. Some countries in the Global South have complained that the West's stockpiling of drugs (as well as related initiatives such as advance purchase agreements with pharmaceutical manufacturers) means that the health of rich, industrialized countries is being protected at the expense of poorer parts of the world who would be unable to acquire the medicines they need during an emergency, either because they are priced out of the market or because global supplies are limited. This raises the issue, to which I return later in the chapter, of whose security is being prioritized, and whether the security of some comes at the expense of others.

Everyday Insecurities and the Global Health Security Agenda

The central claim of securitization theory is that there is no 'fixed list' of security threats – that 'securityness' is established intersubjectively through social processes, and that it is possible, in principle, for new health issues to be added to the security agenda – and perhaps to benefit from the same kinds of exceptional responses that have been seen around pandemics, bioterrorism and (in a different way – see chapter 2) HIV and AIDS. It would be unrealistic, however, to assume that *any* health issue could be successfully securitized – at least if we take the referent object to be the state, as in national security policy. McInnes (2005: 16–17) identifies four factors that appear to play an important role in the likelihood of particular health issues coming to be seen as threats to national and international security: the immediacy of the perceived threat; that the issue is extraordinary or novel in some way; that individuals have restricted ability to limit their exposure to the risk; and that it is picked up by the mass media, who play an important role in generating a sense of fear. Certainly these seem to fit with the types of pandemic threats discussed in chapter 1, and with the risks, whether nefarious or unwitting, emerging from biosciences that were examined in chapter 3. AIDS remains a slightly less comfortable fit – at least in the present day, although at the time that the security implications of AIDS were being most heavily promoted, around the turn of the millennium, perceptions of the immediacy of the threat and of the extraordinary scale of the pandemic were certainly important contributors to the securitization effort. Contagion, however, is central to all of them. There have so far been no indications that security policymakers are willing to view non-communicable diseases (NCDs) in security terms – or even that anyone is willing to try to forward such a case.

If securitization is indeed an important factor in prioritization, there seem to be good reasons to be worried about the fact that the deck seems to be stacked against everyday insecurities arising from health issues that are neither securitized nor readily 'securitizable' – at least if by 'security' we mean threats to the state. There are various methods, all of them in some way problematic, of ranking the most serious health issues that humans across the globe face today. The World Health Organization's 'Top 10 causes of death' provides one possible starting point. In 2016, the most recent year for which this data is available, the top 10 causes of death were (WHO 2018b):

1. Ischaemic heart disease
2. Stroke
3. Chronic obstructive pulmonary disease (COPD)
4. Lower respiratory infections
5. Alzheimer's disease and other dementias
6. Trachea, bronchus, lung cancers
7. Diabetes mellitus
8. Road injury
9. Diarrhoeal diseases
10. Tuberculosis

Only three of these are infectious diseases: lower respiratory infections (such as pneumonia), diarrhoeal diseases, and tuberculosis (TB). Only the latter of these – and then only in its drug-resistant forms – has seriously been discussed in security terms (AIDS, which had previously been in the top 10, has now slipped down the table). The other causes of death in the global top 10 are either injuries (at number 8) or NCDs (numbers 1, 2, 3, 5, 6, 7) linked to a variety of risk factors including living and working conditions, diet, smoking and access to clean water and sanitation. In short, the current global health security agenda bears little relation to what are, statistically speaking, the things that actually kill the most people in the world today – what we might think of as 'everyday insecurities' (Chen and Narasimhan 2003).

The measure of Disability-Adjusted Life Years (DALYs), used by the Global Burden of Disease (GBD) study, which accounts not only for causes of death but also for years of 'healthy life' lost, gives a slightly different ranking, although with ischaemic heart disease and stroke still taking the top two spots (GBD 2015 DALYs and HALE Collaborators 2016: figure 7). What the GBD shows far more clearly than a simple global top 10 of causes of death, however, is the differences between the disease burdens in different places. Crudely put, those in poorer countries are far more likely to die of infectious diseases than those in richer countries, where NCDs – often referred to somewhat simplistically as 'lifestyle diseases' – predominate. This could seem to be a point in favour of securitization as a promoter of global health equity: security policymakers are focusing more on infectious diseases, the major burden of which is carried by the global poor. Alas, this is not the case for two reasons. First, because it is only certain *types* of infectious diseases that have, in practice, made it onto security agendas. What McInnes describes in terms of 'normality' (i.e. that unusual disease events are much more likely than quotidian ones to be seen as security threats) militates against endemic infectious diseases being seen in security terms. Waterborne diseases, for example, which affect those who have no option but to use contaminated water, do not get discussed in security terms. As Davies (2010a: 156) has argued, 'the consequence of bringing infectious disease to the realm of "high politics" has been that only particular diseases have been admitted and many of those that exact the highest morbidity and mortality in the world's poorest places have been excluded and, even, de-emphasized.'

Second, as was shown in chapter 5, the focus of the global health security agenda is on worldwide surveillance and containment to prevent international spread. Cross-border transmission is a crucial factor in whether or not diseases come to be interpreted as security threats. The very definition of Emerging Infectious Diseases, which have captured so much attention amongst security policymakers, refers to diseases that are either newly occurring within a population (for example, new zoonoses), or which are spreading to new geographical areas. Even infectious diseases only take on security relevance when they start crossing borders. West Nile virus, spread by mosquitoes, illustrates this point clearly. As its name suggests, West Nile virus was originally discovered in the 1930s in Africa, specifically in the West Nile district of Uganda. It was subsequently identified in a range of other tropical locations, including India. Its endemicity in these areas was recognized as a public health problem, but not as a security threat. That framing of the disease only came about in 1999, when the first case of West Nile fever was identified in New York City. West Nile was seen as an important exemplar, in those pre-SARS years, of the dangers of international disease transmission in a globalized era. But it was also seen as more than that: it was viewed (remember, that as well as being pre-SARS, this was also pre-9/11) as an important opportunity for learning lessons in advance of a potential bioterrorist attack. As a disease newly introduced into an urban area, and where there was in the early stages considerable confusion about the diagnosis, since West Nile was not on the radar of New York doctors, this was seen as a test of the public health system's ability to identify, investigate and respond to the kind of outbreak that might follow the deliberate release of a pathogen (Covello et al. 2001; Crupi et al. 2003; Henderson et al. 2001). For our purposes, the most plausible lesson to draw from the West Nile example is that diseases that are endemic in the Global South only become security threats once they start to affect new geographical areas (the EID narrative), or that they only become security threats once they start to 'invade' the Global North (and, perhaps, the US in particular).

The fact that infectious diseases that only threaten people living in the developing world struggle to make it onto the global health security agenda is another reason for doubting that the current agenda adequately reflects the disease risks that different populations around the world face, or the domestic health crises that different governments are attempting to address every day. To compound this, the power of the global health security agenda has been such that governments for whom securitized disease threats such as pandemic influenza are not (and arguably should not be) a major health policy priority have been required to devote resources to them. As Thomas Abraham (2011: 809) has argued, 'countries lower down in the global economic and political pecking order are compelled to devote extraordinary attention and resources to issues that might not pose a great threat to them'. Many of these countries lack the basic health infrastructure necessary to deal with the everyday health insecurities their populations face, let alone to prepare for potential future global health emergencies. Understandably, some of them resent the emphasis being placed on a small number of diseases that worry the West.

Even where the Global North and the Global South do have shared perceptions of global health security challenges, security logics can distort the ways in which these come to be tackled. Antimicrobial resistance (AMR) is a prime example. AMR refers to the emergence of pathogens resistant to existing antibiotics, antifungals, antivirals, and antimalarials. There is a broad consensus that this problem is accelerating, with some fearing that in the not-too-distant future we could find ourselves in a 'post-antibiotic era' in which existing medicines are ineffective, and even what are currently seen as minor healthcare procedures become highly risky as a result of the potential for untreatable infection.

In recent years AMR has begun to be increasingly identified in the Global North as a looming health security threat. The UK's Chief Medical Officer, Dame Sally Davies, has been one of the most prominent voices calling for AMR to be recognized as a national security threat to the UK. Outside the UK, political leaders and global institutions have similarly bought in to the framing of AMR as a security problem. As US President, Barack Obama issued an Executive Order in 2014 declaring that 'Combating antibiotic-resistant bacteria is a national security priority' (Obama 2014c). At the same time, organizations such as the WHO have explicitly identified AMR as a threat to global health security (WHO 2014b). Currently, the greatest AMR burden falls in the Global South, where drug-resistant forms of TB and malaria in particular threaten some of the health gains that have been made in the last few decades. The Global North faces a somewhat different issue, mainly focused around hospital-acquired infections and pockets of drug-resistant TB amongst immigrant communities. But in both the North and the South, governments are increasingly recognizing that the threat AMR poses to health and health systems is increasing over time.

In principle, then, this is an area in which there is a clear convergence of interests between the Global North and the Global South. It is to everyone's benefit to find solutions to the AMR challenge. The more difficult political question, however, is around which policy responses should be prioritized. Steven Hoffman and colleagues (2015) have argued that there are three key issues that need to be tackled simultaneously in order to address the global AMR threat: conservation (i.e. reducing the use of antimicrobials and ensuring they are used appropriately, reducing the threat of resistant pathogens emerging); innovation (creating new medicines that can, either temporarily or permanently, circumvent the problem of resistance); and access (ensuring that everyone who needs these medicines has access to them). Perhaps unsurprisingly, the focus from Western governments has been largely on conservation and innovation, which fit a clear logic of attempting to reduce the threat, and of developing technological/pharmacological defences against it. Increasing access to existing antimicrobials, meanwhile, could be seen as being directly contrary to the need for reduced use globally – even though lack of access is arguably a more urgent challenge in low-income countries, where far more people die from not having antimicrobial medicines than currently die from drug-resistant 'superbugs'. In this case, then, even when there is consensus on the problem to be tackled, there can be divergence between what kinds of policy responses are good for the future security of the Global North, and what are good for the current health of people in the Global South.

The Wider Global Health Agenda: Towards Development and Human Security?

It is important to recognize that the global health security agenda and the wider global health agenda are not synonymous. Although security has been a powerful motivating force in global health, it has not driven everything. As we saw with HIV and AIDS in chapter 2, security co-exists with other ways of framing global health, and those other frames have policy effects too.

Although most of the news is bad in this book, there has been some good news over the last three decades, and real health gains have been seen in many parts of the world. The MDGs, discussed in chapter 2 in the context of AIDS, provide some useful (even if selective) benchmarks for judging global health progress. In addition to AIDS, TB and other diseases (MDG6), the MDGs also included goals for reducing child mortality (MDG4) and improving maternal health (MDG5). The global improvements in these indicators were in many ways impressive – even though they were not all met in all countries. Child mortality was reduced by more than half between 1990 and 2015, despite population growth. Some 12.7 million under-5s died in 1990 (United Nations 2015: 5); by 2015, this had been reduced to 6 million – a figure that can hardly be described as a global health 'success', but that did demonstrate the significant investment and effort that had been put into this area, from both national governments and international donors. A similar reduction (of 45%) was seen in maternal mortality between 1990 and 2015, in no small part due to a huge increase in the proportion of births being attended by skilled birth attendants (up from 59% to 71%) (United Nations 2015: 6). Neither child mortality nor maternal mortality were priorities because they were considered national security issues. Instead, investment in these areas was motivated largely by international development concerns. Influential thinkers such as Jeffrey Sachs had made the case for 'investing in health' in order to promote international development, and the MDGs reflected the success of those arguments.

The global figures for health outcomes have shown meaningful improvements across a wide range of health conditions, but global figures can obscure some very large differences in how individual countries have performed. Some national governments put a real emphasis on meeting targets around childhood vaccination, maternal health, HIV prevention and treatment, as well as other pressing health crises. Other governments of equal income level did not. This is a salutary lesson. It is tempting in critical analyses of global health politics to blame the governments of the Global North for health problems in the Global South. But this is often too simplistic: there is plenty of blame to share around. Global South governments also have agency (albeit in many cases constrained by available resources) and also make political choices. They do not always make choices that are good for the health of their populations. Again, this shows the importance of politics to health, in all places and at all levels of governance.

The MDG-driven health and development agenda was broader than the global health security agenda, covering a wider range of health concerns beyond infectious disease and tangibly benefitting a much larger number of people across the globe. But even that agenda was criticized for covering too little. The MDGs were extremely influential in determining the shape of global health programmes and the associated resource flows from 2000 to 2015, but they focused that attention only on three goals. The 'health SDG' (SDG3) was in part an attempt to correct that, according to Buse and Hawkes (2015: 5) constituting a shift towards 'a more holistic vision of health and wellbeing', and crucially including a commitment to Universal Health Coverage.

Both the MDGs and the SDGs show that security is not 'the only game in town'. Health issues can attract international attention and the deployment of resources even when they are not framed as security threats. And the resulting global health agendas can be far more encompassing than the global health security agenda. It is true that even SDG3 is selective in what is covered, as a result of the compromises and trade-offs made in international negotiations over several years (Dodds, Donoghue and Roesch 2016). But it is a significant expansion on the MDG health agenda – and an even more significant expansion on the transnational infectious disease focus of the global health security agenda. The SDGs might even move us somewhere closer to a 'human security' approach.

The concept of human security falls into what Davies (2010b) has called a 'globalist' perspective of health, focusing on health insecurity at the individual level (which she contrasts with the 'statist' perspective, which presents health issues 'as being equivalent to national security threats').

Human security originally rose to prominence in the UNDP's *1994 Human Development Report* which claimed (UNDP 1994: 22–3) that '[t]he idea of human security, though simple, is likely to revolutionize society in the 21st century.' The report went on to say that 'Human security can be said to have two main aspects. It means, first, safety from such chronic disease threats as hunger, disease and repression. And second, it means protection from sudden and harmful disruptions in the patterns of daily life – whether in homes, in jobs or in communities.'

Health security was explicitly identified as one of the components of human security from the outset (along with economic, food, environmental, personal, community and political security) (UNDP 1994: 27–8). Gro Harlem Brundtland, at the time Director-General of the WHO, argued in 2000 that 'More and more governments see good health as a critical element of human security' (Brundtland 2001: 95). And, in contrast with the narrow focus on infectious diseases, human security-based approaches deliberately viewed health in the widest sense, incorporating the full range of communicable and non-communicable diseases and explicitly linking them with poverty and inequality. Thus, those pursuing a human security approach to health would concern themselves *both* with exceptional public health events of the type that are widely seen as national and international security threats ('harmful disruptions in the patterns of everyday life'), *but also* with the more common daily threats to people's health and wellbeing.[14]

The UN explicitly links the SDGs with human security. The UN Trust Fund for Human Security (2018) notes that Agenda 2030 (which set out the SDGs) 'calls for a new approach to address the interconnectivity of today's challenges. To this end, human security provides an effective analytical lens and programming framework.' Deputy Secretary-General Amina J. Mohammed has said that 'The human security approach is instrumental to sustainable development, inclusive peace, justice and the well-being and dignity of all people. It is in fact central to the 2030 Agenda' (UN News 2017).

But it is debatable how widely national governments have seriously adopted human security ways of thinking. The concept was promoted by some states, notably Canada and Japan, in the 1990s, but it has not (so far) succeeded in supplanting more traditional ideas of what security means. This is not to say that the human security project has delivered no change. MacFarlane and Khong (2006: xi) have argued that 'it is too late to put the genie of human security back in the bottle of traditional security analysis', pointing to the broadening of the UN Security Council's agenda – including their discussion of AIDS – as evidence of its impact. There is some truth in this, but it is striking that this broader notion of human security has prospered most where it fitted with pre-existing national security ideas, as AIDS did with established concerns about state failure in sub-Saharan Africa. As Jean-Philippe Théiren (2012: 213) has claimed, 'in countries of the North, human security is often reduced to a foreign policy tool to better manage relations with the countries of the South' – a far cry from its original ideals (see also Davies 2010a: 24).

While governments around the world have (to different degrees) taken up the idea that international development is an important policy aim, including in the foreign policies of governments of the Global North, they have been much more reluctant to radically expand their understandings of health security, which has remained narrowly focused on the national and international security concerns that underpin the global health security agenda discussed in the previous section. To a great extent, then, these health security and international development streams of global health policy and action have existed on separate parallel tracks, involving different ministries at the national level and different institutional structures and processes at the global level. Since disease got onto security agendas, security policymakers have not greatly expanded their view either of the threats their nations face, nor of the policy approaches that might mitigate or prevent those threats.

One optimistic reading of the current relatively narrow scope of health security is that it is still early days: health really only began to be addressed as a matter of security policy in any meaningful sense two decades ago, and it is possible that over time the agenda will indeed broaden to incorporate more health issues, as it has already done in incorporating AMR, for example. Lee and McInnes refer to this as 'a Trojan horse relationship, [in which] public health plays to the traditional concerns of foreign policy to secure a "place at the table". Thus it emphasizes the risks of certain public health issues for national security – such as communicable disease and bio-terror. Once it has secured a seat at the table, it can then begin to promote its own agenda, or enjoy spin-offs and collateral gains.' But, as they go on to note, 'The risk of this strategy is that public health will be unable to expand the agenda beyond the narrow confines of national security. Having bought into another agenda it may lack the political muscle to shape it' (Lee and McInnes 2004: 16).

This is exactly what we have seen in the health security arena in the 15 years since Lee and McInnes wrote that piece. There has been considerable success in persuading security policymakers that they need to pay attention to infectious diseases that cross borders, to extreme health crises such as HIV that may threaten state stability, or to emerging threats from deliberate or accidental releases of pathogens as a result of terrorism or scientific research. But there has been limited success in broadening the agenda beyond this, certainly as regards many of the everyday health crises that affect individuals and communities in the Global South and poorer parts of the Global North.

Insecurity, Globalization and the Meaning of 'Global Health'

Building on the discussion in this chapter and the last, in this section I argue that securitization has not only impacted on the global health agenda but has also profoundly impacted the ways in which 'health' is seen as being 'global'.

The narrative of globalized disease threats has powerfully shaped the ways in which we think of the 'global-ness' of health. In doing so, it has firstly obscured the highly differential risks from infectious diseases faced by different people in different places, and secondly has drawn attention away from other forms of health insecurity that people around the world face every day of their lives. Some insecurities are more readily accepted as 'global' than others, even where there is evidence that everyday health insecurities are also in reality 'global' in many ways, being inextricably entwined with the workings of the global economy.

To begin with infectious diseases that *are* seen as security-relevant, it was shown in chapter 5 that one of the primary ways in which securitization has proceeded, particularly in relation to EIDs, has been through a narrative of globally shared risk – in other words, that globalization has resulted in us living in a global 'community of fate' (Hajer 2003), in which pathogens travel rapidly and practically unstoppably across national borders. Whilst to an extent this discourse is rooted in reality – diseases do travel faster than ever before, even if they always travelled – what it elides is the massively differentiated risks we actually face. Generally, those most affected by such outbreaks are poor people in the Global South. In chapter 5, I linked disease emergence with poverty and inequality. But inequality also plays a large part in determining who will suffer most from cross-border epidemics once they have emerged. To return to the example of the West Africa Ebola epidemic, an outbreak widely constructed as a security threat to the West, 99.88% of total cases and 99.87% of total deaths occurred within Sierra Leone, Liberia and Guinea (CDC 2016). Whilst there was a potential risk of spread to the West (and indeed a handful of cases occurred there), the degree of risk faced by those in the three most affected countries was many magnitudes greater – a fact that was de-emphasized by the appeals to the 'global' nature of the threat. Even within West Africa, the risk of Ebola infection – and for those infected, the risk of death – was highly differentiated. Paul

Farmer (2015) wrote about the risks of infection faced by medical professionals involved in treating Ebola patients. He pointed to the fact that Western doctors were far less likely to become infected than their Sierra Leonean, Guinean or Liberian counterparts. And when something went wrong, almost all infected Western medical professionals were repatriated, treated and survived. Almost all of the West African doctors who were infected, meanwhile, died. For Farmer, this was just one example of a double inequality – 'the grotesque disparities of both risk and outcome' – which exist in what he calls a 'perverse relationship' in which those who face the greatest health risks are precisely those who face the greatest obstacles in accessing care (and, therefore, the worst outcomes). In brutal terms, the lives of some were prioritized over others.

But in this chapter, I have argued that insecurity is not only about pathogens that might cross borders. As we saw in the discussion above, most everyday causes of sickness and death in the world are not the infectious disease-related threats that have been widely securitized. In focusing on infectious diseases as the primary manifestation of 'globalness', other illnesses and their causes – lack of access to safe drinking water and sanitation, inadequate nutrition, bad working conditions, poor air quality, the absence of quality health services, and many more things besides – have become further obscured. Overwhelmingly these problems are seen as being local more than they are global. Certainly it is true they are experienced locally, and that it is changes at the local level that will be needed to address them. National governments have a key role to play here, as do donors pursuing policy goals such as those captured in the SDGs. But 'the causes of the causes' of these health insecurities are, of course, intimately connected to broader inequalities in the global political economy (Labonté, Schrecker and Gupta 2005). It is, as Schrecker and Bambra (2015) have argued, politics that makes us sick. And that includes global politics. And it is the political economy (global and local) that determines whether we have access to water and sanitation, whether our working and living conditions are safe, and all of the other social and economic determinants of health. Prioritization is always political, whether in health or any other sphere of public life. There is no escaping that fact. As a political strategy, securitization undoubtedly has its upsides for those seeking to improve the health of people around the world – particularly in its ability to bring attention and resources. But, as Debra DeLaet (2014: 347) argues

> increased spending on securitized illnesses, most notably HIV/AIDS, has saved lives. Nevertheless, the question remains whether more lives might be saved with fewer downside risks if the resources poured into securitized responses to health challenges were instead used to build public health infrastructure and national health care systems designed to address the poverty-related challenges that are the greatest cause of preventable morbidity and mortality across the globe.

Politically, securitization requires scrutiny in terms of both who is being secured, and from what; and equally importantly, who is not being secured, and from what. Securitization may be smart political strategy. But it is certainly not a panacea for all global health ills. It is not only prioritization that is political: de-prioritization is too. Politics shapes not only what challenges we see, but also which ones we don't.

Conclusion

In questioning the prioritization that securitization produces, we need not argue that resources should not be spent on those diseases that have been securitized. Few would want to argue against attempting to tackle AIDS or Ebola, for example. Neither do we have to abandon the idea of protecting populations in the Global North: that is a perfectly legitimate aim. But we can question why there has not been more success in using these issues as what Lee and McInnes (2004) called a 'Trojan horse' for a broader global health agenda. Why do newborns and their mothers continue to die preventable deaths in Guinea whilst millions of dollars are poured into surveillance systems for emerging diseases, pandemic preparedness, and research and development of vaccines and cures in case of bioterrorist attack?

One answer to this is that health has been captured by a more powerful security politics – just as securitization theorists would predict. Only those issues that can be 'sold' as credible security threats (because they threaten to cross borders into the Global North, or because they threaten to cause unstable states to collapse) have been accepted onto this agenda. But another reason is that the immediately obvious 'global-ness' of these health issues has obscured the ways in which even everyday sources of health insecurity, which at first glance appear to be local, are also connected to 'the global'.

Even if this is right, it would be wrong to understand this as 'politics' distorting what could otherwise be a normatively 'pure' health agenda. Instead, the question is about the *kind* of politics that determines priorities: the dominance of a defensive fear-based security agenda over a more cosmopolitan public health one that might lead to better outcomes for Guinean mothers and babies, and billions of others facing everyday threats to their health around the world.

In the concluding chapter of this book, I consider the question of what a 'pro-health politics' might look like (or, in fact, does look like, since it is already in existence). In chapter 4, I argued that a respect for rights must be part of such a politics. In chapter 5, I argued that such a politics must be preventive, not just reactive – which would include social and economic interventions to tackle the causes of disease emergence. From the discussion in this chapter I add a third requirement: that it must be broad, encompassing a much wider range of health insecurities than are present on the current health security agenda. In the

Conclusion to this book I make the case that two concepts that are too rarely seen in the health security discourse – solidarity and dignity – can help capture these three requirements, and therefore should lie at the heart of a 'pro-health politics'. Further, I argue that this need not undermine efforts to deal with already securitized health threats – indeed, it can enhance them. By focusing not on the security implications of individual pathogens, but rather on the (global and local) determinants of health and access to quality health systems, both everyday insecurities and exceptional public health emergencies can be addressed. While we can never be entirely secure, humans can be made more secure against this wider range of threats than they currently are. The question is, what are we prepared to sacrifice for this level of security?

Conclusion: Towards a Pro-Health Politics

In 2018, the American Council on Science and Health published a book entitled *The Next Plague and How Science Will Stop It* (Berezow et al. 2018). Science, the authors argued, can save us. They pointed to the contribution science has made to identifying new threats, the promise of new vaccine technology, and to other biotechnologies such as synthetic biology. All of these, they said, will help us defeat the 'next plague'. But their claims for science went beyond its direct contribution to our ability to detect and combat infectious disease threats. They claimed also that 'economic and technological advancement', both of which they attribute to science, will make poverty, 'the real underlying cause of many infectious diseases', disappear.

It is not my purpose in this chapter, or in this book, to argue against science. It has brought, and will surely continue to bring, huge improvements in our ability to prevent new outbreaks, to identify them when they do occur, to contain them, and to treat the sick. It is to be hoped that economic and technological advancements will indeed make poverty vanish into thin air – although the evidence to support that claim currently seems slender. Yet science alone is not enough. Science will not automatically promote health equity, address global poverty and inequality, or ensure that people's human rights are respected. Science alone will not even determine what kinds of science get done. Only politics can do that.

In the Introduction to this book, I noted that in global health discussions, politics is often seen as an obstacle to progress. In many ways it is true that it can be. But the answer is not to try to circumvent politics, but rather to embrace it: to pursue a politics that is able to secure populations around the world from disease threats, and at the same time to enable the achievement of other global health goals – not least addressing the vast health inequalities that currently characterize life in the so-called 'global village' and which are the fundamental causes of health insecurity – including many diseases that have come to be seen as security threats. The question is, what *kind* of politics can achieve those things?

Security, Dignity, Solidarity

Just as this book is not arguing against science, neither is it arguing against security. There is nothing wrong with pursuing security: all humans want to be secure, from disease as well as from other things that threaten their wellbeing. A pro-health politics does not need to be an anti-security politics. The two can be mutually reinforcing. Neither is it likely to be a good political strategy to argue against security given that it is already so deeply entrenched in contemporary thinking about global health. As I argued in the Introduction, when it comes to infectious disease, the securitization ship has already sailed. But that does not mean that we should ignore the downsides of a security-driven approach to health and disease. In chapters 4, 5 and 6, I looked at three of these downsides and argued that to correct them, we need a 'pro-health politics' that protects rights, engages in longer-term prevention efforts rather than short-term emergency responses, and that is broad enough to concern itself not only with exceptional events, but also with everyday insecurities. In this section I argue that two concepts that are too rarely seen in the health security discourse – solidarity and dignity – should lie at the heart of such a politics. Pursuing solidarity and dignity can help address both everyday and exceptional health challenges and also help us achieve greater security, for all.

Rather than attempting to defeat the securitization of health, then, we may be better served by pursuing these things to push for a redefinition of *security policy*. Naturally occurring disease outbreaks differ vastly from other contemporary security threats such as terrorism or armed violence – and also from the bioterrorist threats with which pandemics are often lumped together. These differences include the role that social and economic determinants of health play in generating new threats; the massively unequal exposure to the risk of disease and other forms of health insecurity; and the extent to which both individual and collective rights are in play, and sometimes in tension with one another. These differences call for very different kinds of responses to those that we often see around other types of security threats. Currently the focus in health security is on surveillance, preparedness and emergency response: exactly the same approaches that are applied to terrorist attacks or inter-state armed violence. But another kind of response is possible – one that attempts to tackle the root causes of infectious diseases and other health insecurities, to improve access to healthcare and other vital services, rather than focusing narrowly on tracking and containing particular pathogens of international security concern. In such a way, the security concerns to the Global North could be more effectively addressed in a manner that does not so severely distort global health priorities. Other health issues, including endemic and non-communicable diseases, would also benefit as the modality shifted from short-term emergency responses, that are frequently injurious to human rights and civil liberties, towards longer term public health improvement efforts. Both international solidarity and a concern for the dignity of individuals and communities could be brought into security policy in ways that both increase security and reduce the downsides of contemporary security-driven approaches.

The way in which we respond to security threats can and does change over time. Stefan Elbe (2010) has shown some of the ways in which security policies and practices have already been changed by the incorporation of concerns about disease onto the security agenda – leading to what he has called a 'medicalization of security'. To date, however, this has largely been on security's terms: medics and public health experts have sought to assist security policymakers in better defending against exogenous disease threats, through surveillance technologies, preparedness activities, and emergency containment responses. These efforts have for the most part been well-intentioned, and have certainly delivered some health benefits. To date, however, health policy communities have not succeeded in expanding the security agenda beyond a relatively narrow range of pathogenic threats, nor succeeded in arguing for longer term engagements that seek to reduce the likelihood of those threats emerging through attempting to tackle the structural determinants of disease. If this is indeed what Lee and McInnes (2004) called the Trojan horse manoeuvre (see chapter 6), public health advocates remain firmly shut inside the horse.

The reasons for this are mostly obvious. Security trumps health in most national political systems – and certainly does on the global stage. A broadened agenda such as that suggested here would be far more costly, would involve opening up wider discussions about the roots of global inequalities that the most powerful nations may have a desire to avoid, and may well be unpopular amongst electorates in donor countries who are, in general, far more willing to support spending on national security than on international aid, let alone a more fundamental rebalancing of the global economy. So, are there any realistic prospects of shifting the debate?

AIDS may offer something of an insight here – even if it is in many ways an imperfect model. As was discussed in chapter 2, AIDS did come to be seen by some powerful states as a threat to international peace and security, particularly once it came to be linked with concerns around state failure in sub-Saharan Africa. But alongside this, a vibrant global advocacy movement has simultaneously pursued other ways of persuading policymakers to act, including through framing the pandemic as a threat to international development and human rights. Arguments about the importance of international solidarity and the dignity of PLWHA have co-existed with the security discourse – indeed for most of the history of AIDS they have been more prominent. To be sure, PLWHA have suffered – and in some places continue to suffer – more than their fair share of stigma, discrimination, human rights abuses and indignity. But rather than accept this as the price of political attention, AIDS advocates and activists have made huge efforts to shift the terms of the debate, away from the view that PLWHA represent a threat to the wider community and even to entire states, and instead onto the ground of human rights and global justice, stressing the need for dignity, representation and voice for affected communities, and the moral obligation on richer governments to show solidarity by helping poorer ones to address their domestic epidemics. This has been a rocky road, beset with difficulties. And it is certainly not the case that current global policy responses to AIDS are unproblematic. Although infection rates have been reduced and many more people now have access to treatment than ever before, the right to health of many PLWHA has still not been realized. Nevertheless, the history of global responses to AIDS at least offers an indication that a less exclusionary approach to addressing security concerns around infectious disease is possible – and can be effective.

Whether this can translate to other health issues is an open question. In chapter 2, I discussed some of the things that set AIDS apart from the other pathogenic threats discussed in this book. It is a long-wave event rather than a short-term epidemic emergency. Contagion is fuelled by stigma and discrimination, and combatting those things is widely understood as being essential to an effective public health response. The perceived security implications were – at least from the mid-1990s onwards – less about cross-border contagion and more about the disease's impact on state capacity. Partly as a result of organizing in the communities in which it was first detected, there was from the very earliest days of the epidemic a vibrant and committed activist movement. AIDS subsequently attracted many high-profile celebrity advocates, from Princess Diana to Bono, who were able to contribute to securing and maintaining its place on high-level political agendas. In some ways, then, AIDS may be *sui generis*. But while it may not be possible to replicate the story of AIDS activism for other health issues, what we can take from the global AIDS response is the importance of political action and engagement. It was the politicization of AIDS that delivered the global solidarity that we have seen, and which allowed for the foregrounding of the rights of PLWHA as a fundamental requirement of the global response. This solidarity beyond national borders and concern with the importance of dignity to an effective public health response has been essential both in promoting justice *and* addressing security concerns.

Returning to the question of prioritization, we can see one downside of the (relative) success of AIDS: that AIDS has – both internationally and domestically within many states – dominated global health spending to an extent that could be seen as disproportionate (see chapter 2). If global health spending is a zero-sum game, then successfully repeating AIDS advocacy elsewhere could have the same effect, of generating a prioritization of one disease at the expense of others. A broader approach, that included serious efforts aimed at strengthening health systems rather than seeking to identify and control particular pathogens, would of course require a completely different level of resourcing. If we wanted to make a more concerted effort to strengthen health systems, poorer countries would need, amongst other things, help with building infrastructure; reduced prices for vaccines, medications, diagnostics and other medical equipment;

and vastly more health personnel. A more holistic and preventive approach to health insecurity would also need investment not only in health systems, but also in water, sanitation, housing, education, and many other things. It would need global poverty to be addressed. Each of these on its own is a difficult and hugely costly challenge.

The questions for Western governments, who proclaim the need to address global disease threats but have not to date shown the willingness to spend the amounts of money required to achieve that, are those with which I began this book: How much security do we feel that we need? And what are we prepared to sacrifice in order to get it?

There is currently a disjuncture between words and deeds. Governments proclaim their desire both to protect themselves and to achieve global health security, but are reluctant to do what it would really take to deliver on that promise – indeed they often act in ways that are contrary to those goals. This is why politics is important: political engagement is the way in which governments can be held to account, perceptions of interest can gradually be shifted, and new pathways of response opened up. Currently, however, there is a trend in the other direction: towards an attempted depoliticization of global health, backed by an appeal to technocratic expertise and empirical evidence as 'more rational' (and perhaps less controversial) bases on which to make policy. In the next section I argue that although expertise and evidence are of course important, this is an approach that fails to offer the hope of a more progressive global health politics – something that would enhance rather than undermine national and global health security.

Against Depoliticization: Towards a Pro-Health Politics

There is nothing wrong with valuing medical or public health expertise and evidence. They are important and should be at the heart of all good health policymaking. Scepticism about experts has led to many policy wrong turns. Rigorous research, translated into effective interventions and policy, can and has had an enormous effect on improving health outcomes for populations around the world. This does not, however, mean that there is no place for politics.

In health policy discussions, 'politicized' is often used to denote the opposite of rational, evidence-based decision-making (e.g. Schwartz and Rosen 2004). But depoliticization is not a path to some mythical state of pure rationality. Even if we wanted to exclude politics from decision-making, we couldn't. Politics is an essential part of creating policy, both good and bad. As Justin Parkhurst (2017) has argued, what is required is not to use evidence to depoliticize policymaking, but rather to utilize politics to ensure the good use of evidence. Politics, evidence and expertise are not inherently in tension. Evidence and expertise become important in changing real people's lives only when used for a political purpose.

Even when supposedly non-political technocratic mechanisms are created, politics inevitably finds its way back in. Amy Barnes and Garrett Brown (2011) looked at the Global Fund – a body ostensibly designed to make decisions about AIDS, TB and malaria financing on a purely rational and technical basis and to exclude political considerations from its funding decisions. Unsurprisingly, they found that in practice it does no such thing. Politics continually re-asserts itself. What is more, they argued that the veneer of depoliticization can obscure this politics in ways that are damaging, reducing transparency and undermining accountability. There are, then, good normative reasons for wanting politics to be part of the policymaking process: 'it can only be through some form of political discourse, negotiation, and public-reason formation that a system of global health governance can claim to determine legitimately "who gets what, when and how?" ' (Barnes and Brown 2011: 74).

At the same time, 'evidence' is itself a product of political decisions, and 'evidence-based policy' is itself a political project. An enormous amount of work exists on the politics of knowledge that explores this. Some research projects are funded and others aren't. Certain kinds of data are collected and other kinds aren't. Some types of findings translate more easily than others into palatable policy recommendations. Politics comes in at every stage of the research process (Barnes and Parkhurst 2014). But again, this is best viewed as a positive. Gorik Ooms (2016) has argued that 'global health research is essentially a normative undertaking' and that we need 'to acknowledge that a purely empirical evidence-based approach is a fiction.' Subsequent commentators on Ooms' argument agreed. Ilona Kickbusch (2016), for example, said that 'It is time to acknowledge that expert-based technocratic approaches are no less political.' This, as Ooms rightly says, makes it incumbent on us to be explicit about the political nature of our analyses. It also requires us to be reflexive about our own scholarly activities and biases (Rushton 2015). Researchers and experts in global health politics, just as in any other social science field, cannot avoid bringing their preconceptions, prejudices and political commitments with them. Although we might know this in theory, we are often guilty of failing to admit to it in practice, often falling into the trap of presenting our arguments as objective truths. There is a need to be explicit that working in global health is itself a political activity.

Can health professionals and researchers really hope to play a role in shifting security policy debates – or will they always be subservient to the real movers and shakers of national and international politics? History suggests that in some cases they can create change – indeed that experts in health might even have certain advantages when it comes to being taken seriously. The medical peace movement is one clear example. The *New England Journal of Medicine*'s publication of a series of articles on 'The Medical Consequences of Thermonuclear War' in 1962 was a momentous intervention by medical researchers into security policy, taking on – at the height of the Cold War – the very cornerstone of the superpowers' security policies. Whilst these articles did not lead to the immediate abandonment of nuclear weapons, they did fundamentally change the terms of the debate. Over half a century later, ICAN, the International Campaign to Abolish Nuclear Weapons, was awarded the Nobel Peace Prize for its success in bringing to the UN General Assembly a treaty on the prohibition of nuclear weapons. ICAN grew out of the medical peace movement, its origins in a campaign launched in 2006 by International Physicians for the Prevention of Nuclear War (IPPNW).

Although the esteem in which they are held has arguably waned over the years in some countries (Schlesinger 2002), in most societies health professionals continue to have a high social standing which they may be able to leverage for policy impact. Such an impact needs to be pursued, not assumed, however. Claiming that those with medical expertise can be influential is not the same as claiming that health will always be prioritized. History doesn't bear out that assertion at all. Governments frequently make choices that are contrary to good health evidence, and assuming that health will 'speak for itself' and be valued in a way that is decisive in policy debates could in fact be counterproductive if it steers us away from strategic political engagements. Global health scholars and practitioners should be pursuing those engagements, forwarding the case for a broader vision of health security that protects rights, seeks to prevent disease, and recognizes the wide varieties of different health insecurities that people around the world face. Health professionals need to argue for dignity and solidarity to have a far more prominent place in global and national health policymaking. In doing so, they should not act alone. A broader movement, including real public participation, is required to effectively forward a new pro-health politics that pursues *repoliticization* rather than depoliticization. Once again, the AIDS movement – noisy, demanding, sometimes confrontational – offers some interesting examples of what such an engagement might look like. It is that kind of commitment and that kind of politics that is needed to challenge and change security elites. Security politics is rarely democratic or inclusive unless democracy and inclusion are demanded.

Bernard Crick (1962: 199) concluded his classic book *In Defence of Politics* with a quote that is a salutary reminder for all of us concerned with health: 'The truth is that there is nothing above politics' (Crick 1962: 198–9).

Notes

1 Whereas the Copenhagen School sees security threats as those that pose an 'existential threat' to the state, the history of disease and security calls this into question. It is not just mortality or the threat of societal collapse that has made security policymakers interested in disease. The economic costs of major outbreaks have also, for example, been a particularly prominent cause of security concern.

2 For a more detailed analysis of the ways in which security ideas fed into the revision of the IHR, see Davies, Kamradt-Scott and Rushton (2015: chapter 1).

3 This is not to say that there was a parliamentary consensus on the issue. Senator Sarah Hanson-Young of the Green Party, for example, spoke passionately against what she described as the 'mean, cruel and incredibly selfish' government position (Senate Hansard 2014).

4 The IHR Review Committee also singled Ghana out for praise, noting that 'Ghana kept its borders open, which proved to be critical in facilitating the flow of essential supplies and personnel to the affected countries' (Review Committee on the Role of the International Health Regulations (2005) in the Ebola Outbreak and Response 2016: 46).

5 The panel that investigated the incident came to the conclusion that the boxes had most probably been placed in the store in the 1960s or 1970s, but were unable to determine precisely when (Blue Ribbon Panel 2017: 8).

6 The report was in fact submitted to the Secretary of State for Social Services in December 1978, but was withheld from the public until the completion of a legal case.

7 There is no complete global list of BSL-4 labs. Work by the Federation of American Scientists in 2010–11 resulted in a list of forty-two BSL-4 facilities worldwide (twelve of which were in the US), although this may now be outdated. See https://fas.org/programs/bio/biosafetylevels.html

8 Although the biosecurity risks posed by the potential misuse of gain of function-type work was what captured much of the attention, there were also biosafety concerns at play in the debate over the potential for an accidental release of such potentially deadly pathogens.

9 The DoD's plans were later shelved (Petro 2004).

10 There are two draft codes of ethics currently under discussion: one for Europe and one for North America. See https://diybio.org/codes/

11 See http://ask.diybio.org

12 The following rights are specifically listed: the right to life; freedom from torture, cruel, inhuman or degrading treatment or punishment, and from medical or scientific experimentation without free consent; freedom from slavery or involuntary servitude; the right not be imprisoned for contractual debt; the right not to be convicted or sentenced to a heavier penalty by virtue of retroactive criminal legislation; the right to recognition as a person before the law; and freedom of thought, conscience and religion.

13 Sao Tome and Principe (16%), Nepal (22%), Burundi (25%), Central African Republic (27%), Equatorial Guinea (27%), Gambia (27%), Andorra (29%), Somalia (29%), Benin (30%), Congo (31%), Mauritania (32%), Djibouti (33%), South Sudan (34%), Vanuatu (35%), Comoros (37%), Mali (40%).

14 'Critical Security Studies' approaches, which focus on the idea of security as emancipation (Booth 1991, 2007) and seek to address the threats faced by 'real people in real places' (Bilgic 2015), offer a similar attempt to redefine what security is *for*, and therefore what kinds of issues might be deemed threats to security. João Nunes (2014: 8) has argued that an emancipatory approach to health security could be a route to overcoming the 'absence [in existing health security discourse] of an explicit commitment to ... normative judgement'.

For Nunes (2014: 120), realizing health security understood as emancipation would require 'the transformation of the structures and relations that entail systematic inequality, disadvantage, and vulnerability, thus resulting in different forms of harm.' In doing so, policymakers would be required to engage with a far wider range of vulnerabilities and threats than the current health security agenda does: they would need to examine the many direct and indirect threats to individuals' health around the world – not only pathogens that threaten to cross national borders.

References

Aaltola, Mika. 2012a. *Understanding the Politics of Pandemic Scares: An introduction to global politosomatics*. Abingdon: Routledge.

Aaltola, Mika. 2012b. 'Contagious insecurity: war, SARS and global air mobility', *Contemporary Politics* 18(1): 53–70.

Abraham, Thomas. 2011. 'The chronicle of a disease foretold: pandemic H1N1 and the construction of a global health security threat', *Political Studies* 59(4): 797–812.

Abrahamsen, Rita. 2005. 'Blair's Africa: the politics of securitization and fear', *Alternatives* 30(1): 55–80.

Achenbach, Joel. 2014. 'Paul Farmer on Ebola: "This isn't a natural disaster, this is the terrorism of poverty" ', *Washington Post* Achenblog, 6 October. Available at: https://www.washingtonpost.com/news/achenblog/wp/2014/10/06/paul-farmer-on-ebola-this-isnt-a-natural-disaster-this-is-the-terrorism-of-poverty

African Union. 2014. Press release: African Union's Executive Council urges lifting of travel restrictions related to Ebola outbreak. 8 September. Available at: https://www.au.int/web/en/pressreleases/27043/african-union's-executive-council-urges-lifting-travel-restrictions-related

Aginam, Obijifor. 2003. 'The nineteenth century colonial fingerprints on public health diplomacy: A postcolonial view', *Law, Social Justice and Global Development Journal* 1. Available at: http://www2.warwick.ac.uk/fac/soc/law/elj/lgd/2003_1/aginam

Aiello, Allison. 2014. 'Ebola as an Instrument of Discrimination'. Robert Wood Johnson Foundation 'Cultures of Health' blog, 21 November. Available at: https://www.rwjf.org/en/blog/2014/11/ebola_as_an_instrume.html

Allin, N.E. 1988. 'The AIDS pandemic: international travel and immigration restrictions and the World Health Organization's response', *Virginia Journal of International Law* 28: 1043–64.

American Association for the International Commission of Jurists. 1985. *Siracusa Principles on the Limitation and Derogation Provisions in the International Covenant on Civil and Political Rights*. New York: American Association for the International Commission of Jurists. Available at: https://www.icj.org/wp-content/uploads/1984/07/Siracusa-principles-ICCPR-legal-submission-1985-eng.pdf

Amon, Joseph J. 2014. 'Health security and/or human rights?' in Simon Rushton and Jeremy Youde (eds.), *The Routledge Handbook of Global Health Security*. Abingdon: Routledge.

Anderson, Emma-Louise and Alexander Beresford. 2016. 'Infectious injustice: the political foundations of the Ebola crisis in Sierra Leone', *Third World Quarterly* 37(3): 468–86.

Andrus, Jon Kim, Ximena Aguilera, Otavio Oliva and Sylvain Aldighieri. 2010. 'Global health security and the International Health Regulations', *BMC Public Health* 10(Supp.1): S2.

Annan, Kofi. 2001. 'Transcript of Press Conference by Secretary-General Kofi Annan at Headquarters, 27 June 2001'. SG/SM/7865. Available at: http://www.un.org/News/Press/docs/2001/sgsm7865.doc.htm

Anonymous. 2010. 'The shutting up infected houses', *Public Health Ethics* 3(1): 4–12.

Armour, Stephanie. 2016. 'White House to shift about $500 million for fighting Ebola to combating Zika', *Wall Street Journal*, 6 April. Available at: https://www.wsj.com/articles/white-house-to-shift-about-500-million-for-fighting-ebola-to-combating-zika-1459962865

Avert. 2017. 'Donor funding for HIV and AIDS'. Available at: https://www.avert.org/professionals/hiv-around-world/global-response/funding

Bajekal, Naina. 2014. 'Why Ebola hasn't really spread across West Africa', *Time*, 22 October. Available at: http://time.com/3528833/ebola-spread-west-africa/

Bambra, Clare, Debbie Fox and Alex Scott-Samuel. 2005. 'Towards a politics of health', *Health Promotion International* 20(2): 187–93.

Bankoff, Gregory. 2001. 'Rendering the world unsafe: 'vulnerability' as Western discourse', *Disasters* 25(1): 19–35.

Barnes, Amy and Garrett Wallace Brown. 2011. 'The global fund to fight AIDS, tuberculosis and malaria: expertise, accountability and the depoliticisation of global health governance', in Owain Williams and Simon Rushton (eds.), *Partnerships and Foundations in Global Health Governance*. Basingstoke: Palgrave Macmillan.

Barnes, Amy and Justin Parkhurst. 2014. 'Can global health policy be depoliticized? A critique of global calls for evidence-based policy', in Garrett W. Brown, Gavin Yamey and Sarah Wamala (eds.), *The Handbook of Global Health Policy*. Oxford: Wiley Blackwell.

Barnett, Tony 2006. 'A long-wave event. HIV/AIDS, politics, governance and "security": sundering the intergenerational bond?', *International Affairs* 82(2): 297–313.

Barnett, Tony and Gwin Prins. 2005. '*HIV/AIDS and security: fact, fiction and evidence. A report to UNAIDS*'. London: LSEAIDS. Available at: http://www.lse.ac.uk/researchAndExpertise/units/mackinder/pdf/aidsReport.pdf

Bashford, Alison. 2004. *Imperial Hygiene: A Critical History of Colonialism, Nationalism and Public Health*. Basingstoke: Palgrave Macmillan.

Bayer, Ronald. 2007. 'The continuing tensions between individual rights and public health. Talking Point on public health versus civil liberties', *EMBO Reports* 8(12): 1099–103.

BBC News. 2014. 'Ebola crisis: Senegal defends Guinea border closure', 22 August. Available at: http://www.bbc.co.uk/news/world-africa-28893835

Ben Ouargrham-Gormley, Sonia. 2012. 'Barriers to bioweapons: intangible obstacles to proliferation', *International Security* 36(4): 80–114.

Berezow, Alex, Hank Campbell, Julianna LeMieux and Steve Schow. 2018. *The Next Plague and How Science Will Stop It*. New York: American Council on Science and Health.

Bilgic, Ali. 2015. ' "Real people in real places": conceptualizing power for emancipatory security through Tahrir', *Security Dialogue* 46(3): 272–90.

Blue Ribbon Panel to Review the 2014 Smallpox (Variola) Virus Incident on the NIH Campus. 2017. Bethesda, MD: National Institutes of Health.

Booth, Ken. 1991. 'Security and emancipation', *Review of International Studies* 17(4): 313–26.

Booth, Ken. 2007. *Theory of World Security*. Cambridge: Cambridge University Press.

Brandt, Allan M. 2013. 'How AIDS invented global health', *New England Journal of Medicine* 368: 2149–52.

Brown, Gordon. 2005. 'Spend now, save lives', *The Guardian*, 5 June. Available at: https://www.theguardian.com/politics/2005/jun/05/internationalaidanddevelopment.development

Brown, Theodore M., Marcos Cueto and Elizabeth Fee. 2006. 'The World Health Organization and the transition from "international" to "global" public health', *American Journal of Public Health* 96(1): 62–72.

Brundtland, Gro Harlem. 2001. 'Statement by Dr Gro Harlem Brundtland, Director General WHO, to the Fifth Global Conference on Health Promotion, Mexico City, 5 June 2000', *Health Promotion International* 16(1): 95–8.

Burnett, James C., Rekha G. Panchal, M. Javad Aman and Sina Bavari. 2005. 'The rapidly advancing field of biodefense benefits many other, critical public health concerns', *Discovery Medicine* 5(28): 371–7.

Buse, Kent and Sarah Hawkes. 2015. 'Health in the sustainable development goals: ready for a paradigm shift?', *Globalization and Health* 11: 13. DOI 10.1186/s12992-015-0098-8.

Buzan, Barry, Ole Waever and Jaap de Wilde. 1998. *Security: A New Framework for Analysis*. Boulder, CO: Lynne Rienner.

Campbell Bartoletti, Susan. 2015. *Terrible Typhoid Mary: A True Story of the Deadliest Cook in America*. New York: Houghton Mifflin.

Canas, Linda C., Kenton Lohman, Julie A. Pavlin, et al. 2000. 'The Department of Defense Laboratory-Based Global Influenza Surveillance System', *Military Medicine* 165(Supp.2): 52–5.

Carlson, Robert. 2003. 'The pace and proliferation of biological technologies', *Biosecurity and Bioterrorism* 1(2): 203–14.

Casadevall, Arturo and Michael J. Imperiale. 2014. 'Risks and benefits of gain-of-function experiments with pathogens of pandemic potential, such as influenza virus: a call for a science-based discussion', *mBio* 5(4): e01730-14.

CDC (Centers for Disease Control and Prevention). 2016. 'Ebola (Ebola Virus Disease). Case Counts'. Available at: https://www.cdc.gov/vhf/ebola/history/2014-2016-outbreak/case-counts.html

CDC (Centers for Disease Control and Prevention). 2018. 'Stockpile Products'. Available at: https://www.cdc.gov/phpr/stockpile/products.htm

CDC (Centers for Disease Control and Prevention). n.d. 'Global Disease Detection (GDD) Program'. Available at: https://www.cdc.gov/globalhealth/healthprotection/gdd/index.html

Chan, Jennifer. 2015. *Politics in the Corridor of the Dying: AIDS Activism and Global Health Governance*. Baltimore, MD: Johns Hopkins University Press.

Chan, Lai-Ha, Lucy Chen and Jin Xu. 2010. 'China's engagement with global health diplomacy: was SARS a watershed?', *PLOS Medicine* 7(4): e1000266.

Chan, Margaret. 2009. 'World now at the start of 2009 influenza pandemic'. Statement to the press by WHO Director-General Dr Margaret Chan, 11 June 2009. Available at: http://www.who.int/mediacentre/news/statements/2009/h1n1_pandemic_phase6_20090611/en/

Chan, Margaret. 2014. 'WHO Director-General addresses UN Security Council on Ebola', 18 September. Available at: http://www.who.int/dg/speeches/2014/security-council-ebola/en/

Check Hayden, Erika. 2011. 'Biodefence since 9/11: the price of protection'. *Nature* 477: 150–2.

Chen, Lincoln and Vasant Narasimhan. 2003. 'Human security and global health', *Journal of Human Development* 4(2): 181–90.

CIA (Central Intelligence Agency). 1987. Sub-Saharan Africa: Implications of the AIDS Pandemic. SNIE 70/1–87 (approved for release May 2001). Available at: https://www.cia.gov/library/readingroom/docs/DOC_0000579295.pdf

Clapper, James R. 2016. *Worldwide Threat Assessment of the US Intelligence Community*. Washington, DC: Senate Armed Services Committee. Available at: https://www.dni.gov/files/documents/SASC_Unclassified_2016_ATA_SFR_FINAL.pdf

Cockerham, Geoffrey B. and William C. Cockerham. 2010. *Health and Globalization*. Cambridge: Polity.

Cohen, Deborah and Philip Carter. 2010. 'Conflicts of interest: WHO and the pandemic flu "conspiracies" ', *BMJ* 340: 1274–9.

Cohen, Jon, 2016. 'Patient Zero no more', *Science* 351(6277): 1013.

Coker, Richard and Alan Ingram. 2006. 'Passports and pestilence: migration, security and contemporary border control of infectious diseases', in Alison Bashford (ed.), *Medicine at the Border: Disease, Globalization and Security, 1850 to the Present.* Basingstoke: Palgrave Macmillan.

Commission on Macroeconomics and Health. 2002. *Global Public Goods for Health: Report of Working Group 2 of the Commission on Macroeconomics and Health.* Geneva: WHO. Available at: http://apps.who.int/iris/bitstream/handle/10665/42518/9241590106.pdf?sequence=1

Cooper, Andrew F., John J. Kirton and Ted Schrecker. 2007. 'Toward innovation in global health governance', in Andrew F. Cooper, John J. Kirton and Ted Schrecker (eds.), *Governing Global Health: Challenge, Response, Innovation.* Aldershot: Ashgate.

Covello, Vincent T., Richard G. Peters, Joseph G. Wojtecki and Richard C. Hyde. 2001. 'Risk communication, the West Nile Virus epidemic, and bioterrorism: responding to the communication challenges posed by the intentional or unintentional release of a pathogen in an urban setting', *Journal of Urban Health* 78(2): 382–91.

Cravioto, Alejando, Claudio F. Lanata, Daniele S. Lantagne and G. Balakrish Nair. 2011. Final Report of the Independent Panel of Experts on the Cholera Outbreak in Haiti. Available at: http://www.un.org/News/dh/infocus/haiti/UN-cholera-report-final.pdf

Crick, Bernard. 1962. *In Defence of Politics.* London: Penguin.

Crupi, Robert S., Deborah S. Asnis, Christopher C. Lee, Thomas Santucci, Mark J. Marino and Bruce J. Flanz. 2003. 'Meeting the challenge of bioterrorism: lessons learned from West Nile virus and anthrax', *American Journal of Emergency Medicine* 21(1): 77–9.

Daily Telegraph. 1983. ' "Gay Plague" may lead to blood ban on homosexuals'. *Daily Telegraph*, 2 May.

Dalby, Simon. 1998. 'Reading "The Coming Anarchy"', in Simon Dalby, Paul Routledge and Gearóid Ó Tuathail (eds.), *The Geopolitics Reader.* London: Routledge.

Davies, Sara E. 2010a. *Global Politics of Health.* Cambridge: Polity.

Davies, Sara E. 2010b. 'What contribution can International Relations make to the evolving global health agenda?', *International Affairs* 86(5): 1167–90.

Davies, Sara E. 2014. 'Internet surveillance and disease outbreaks', in Simon Rushton and Jeremy Youde (eds.), *The Routledge Handbook of Global Health Security*. Abingdon: Routledge.

Davies, Sara E., Adam Kamradt-Scott and Simon Rushton. 2015. *Disease Diplomacy: International Norms and Global Health Security*. Baltimore, MD: Johns Hopkins University Press.

DeLaet, Debra. 2014. 'Whose interests is securitization serving?', in Simon Rushton and Jeremy Youde (eds.), *The Routledge Handbook of Global Health Security*. Abingdon: Routledge.

Department of Health and Human Services. 2009. *Biosafety in Microbiological and Biomedical Laboratories (BMBL), 5th Edition*. Washington, DC: Department of Health and Human Services. Available at: https://www.cdc.gov/biosafety/publications/bmbl5/bmbl.pdf

Dodds, Felix, Ambassador David Donoghue and Jimena Leiva Roesch. 2016. *Negotiating the Sustainable Development Goals*. London: Routledge.

Doshi, Peter. 2011. 'The elusive definition of pandemic influenza', *Bulletin of the World Health Organization* 89: 532–8.

Dunn, Kevin C. 2004. 'Fear of a black planet: anarchy anxieties and postcolonial travel to Africa', *Third World Quarterly* 25(3): 483–99.

Elbe, Stefan. 2003. *Strategic Implications of HIV/AIDS*. Adelphi Papers, no. 357. Oxford: Oxford University Press.

Elbe, Stefan. 2005. 'AIDS, Security, Biopolitics', *International Relations* 19(4): 403–19.

Elbe, Stefan. 2010. *Security and Global Health*. Cambridge: Polity.

Elbe, Stefan. 2011. 'Should health professionals play the global health security card?', *Lancet*, 378(9787): 220–1.

Elbe, Stefan. 2018. *Pandemics, Pills, and Politics: Governing Global Health Security*. Baltimore, MD: Johns Hopkins University Press.

Elbe, Stefan, Anne Roemer-Mahler and Christopher Long. 2015. 'Medical countermeasures for national security: a new government role in the pharmaceuticalization of society', *Social Science and Medicine* 131: 263–71.

Emanuel, Ezekiel J. 2012. 'PEPFAR and maximizing the effects of global health assistance', *JAMA* 307(19): 2097–100.

Enemark, Christian. 2005. 'The bird flu menace in east Asia', *Security Challenges*, 1(1): 7–10.

Enemark, Christian. 2017. *Biosecurity Dilemmas: Dreaded Diseases, Ethical Responses, and the Health of Nations*. Washington, DC: Georgetown University Press.

England, Roger, 2007. 'Are we spending too much on HIV?', *BMJ* 334: 344.

Evans, David K., Markus Goldstein and Anna Popova. 2015. 'Health-care worker mortality and the legacy of the Ebola epidemic', *The Lancet Global Health* 3(8): e439–e440.

Evans, Tim. 2018. 'Moving away from panic and neglect: a big step forward on pandemic preparedness and response'. *World Bank Investing in Health blog, 7 June*. Available at: http://blogs.worldbank.org/health/node/888

Farmer, Paul. 1999. *Infections and Inequalities: The Modern Plagues*, 2nd edn. Berkeley, CA: University of California Press.

Farmer, Paul. 2003. *Pathologies of Power: Health, Human Rights and the New War on the Poor*. Berkeley, CA: University of California Press.

Farmer, Paul. 2015. 'The caregivers' disease', *London Review of Books* 37(10): 25–8.

Fidler, David P. 2001. 'The globalization of public health: the first 100 years of international health diplomacy', *Bulletin of the World Health Organization* 79: 842–9.

Fidler, David P. 2003a. *SARS, Governance and the Globalization of Disease*. Basingstoke: Palgrave Macmillan.

Fidler, David P. 2003b. 'SARS: political pathology of the first post-Westphalian pathogen', *Journal of Medicine, Law & Ethics* 31: 485–505.

Fidler, David P. and Lawrence O. Gostin. 2007. *Biosecurity in the Global Age: Biological Weapons, Public Health, and the Rule of Law*. Palo Alto, CA: Stanford University Press.

Field, Andrea. 2012. 'HIV-positive Haitians at Guantánamo Bay', *Guantanamo Public Memory* Project blog, 10 August. Available at: http://blog.gitmomemory.org/2012/04/10/hiv-positive-haitians-at-guantanamo-bay/

Fineberg, Harvey. 2014. 'Pandemic preparedness and response — lessons from the H1N1 influenza of 2009', *New England Journal of Medicine* 370(14): 1335–42.

Florin, Dominique. 1996. 'Barriers to evidence based policy', *BMJ* 313: 894.

Flynn, Daniel and Stephanie Nebehay. 2014. 'Aid workers ask where was WHO in Ebola outbreak?', *Reuters*, 5 October. Available at: https://www.reuters.com/article/us-health-ebola-who/aid-workers-ask-where-was-who-in-ebola-outbreak-idUSKCN0HU03Q20141005

Foege, William. 2000. 'Surveillance, eradication and control: successes and failures', in Jim Whitman (ed.), *The Politics of Emerging and Resurgent Infectious Diseases*. Basingstoke: Macmillan.

Foucault, Michel. 2014. 'The politics of health in the eighteenth century'. Trans. Richard Lynch, *Foucault Studies* 18: 113–27.

France, David. 2016. *How to Survive a Plague: The Story of How Activists and Scientists Tamed AIDS*. New York: Picador.

Franco, Crystal and Tara Kirk Sell. 2011. 'Federal Agency biodefense funding, FY2011–FY2012', *Biosecurity and Bioterrorism* 9(2): 117–37.

Frischknecht, Friedrich. 2003. 'The history of biological warfare', *Science & Society* 4: S47–S52.

G8. 2005. The Gleneagles Communiqué. Available at: http://www.g8.utoronto.ca/summit/2005gleneagles/communique.pdf

Gallo, Robert C. 2006. 'A reflection on HIV/AIDS research after 25 years', *Retrovirology* 3: 72.

Garrett, Laurie. 1994. *The Coming Plague*. London: Atlantic Books.

Gates, Bill. 2015. 'The next epidemic – lessons from Ebola', *New England Journal of Medicine* 372: 1381–4.

Gates, Bill. 2018. 'Gene editing for good: how CRISPR could transform global development', *Foreign Affairs* May/June. Available at: https://www.foreignaffairs.com/articles/2018-04-10/gene-editing-good?cid=nlc-emc-paywall-free-reading-bill-gates-a-20180411

GBD 2015 Mortality and Causes of Death Collaborators. 2016. 'Global, regional, and national life expectancy, all-cause mortality, and cause-specific mortality for 249 causes of death, 1980–2015: a systematic analysis for the Global Burden of Disease Study 2015', *The Lancet* 388: 1459–544.

GBD 2015 DALYs and HALE Collaborators. 2016. 'Global, regional, and national disability-adjusted life-years (DALYs) for 315 diseases and injuries and healthy life expectancy (HALE), 1990–2015: a systematic analysis for the Global Burden of Disease Study 2015', *The Lancet* 388: 1603–58.

Geffen, Nathan. 2010. *Debunking Delusions: The Inside Story of the Treatment Action Campaign*. Johannesburg: Jacana Media.

Gerstein, Daniel M. 2016. 'How genetic editing became a national security threat', *Bulletin of the Atomic Scientists*, 25 April. Available at: http://thebulletin.org/how-genetic-editing-became-national-security-threat9362

Ghinai, Isaac, Chris Willott, Ibrahim Dadari and Heidi Larson. 2013. 'Listening to the rumours: what the northern Nigeria polio vaccine boycott can tell us ten years on', *Global Public Health* 8(10): 1138–50.

GHSA (Global Health Security Agenda). 2014. 'Global Health Security Agenda: action packages'. Available at: https://www.cdc.gov/globalhealth/security/pdf/ghsa-action-packages_24-september-2014.pdf

Gill, Peter. 2006. *Body Count: How They Turned AIDS into a Catastrophe*. London: Profile.

Gilman, Sander L. 2010. 'Moral panic and pandemics', *The Lancet* 375(9729): 1866–7.

Global Fund. 2017. *Results Report 2017*. Geneva: Global Fund. Available at: https://reliefweb.int/report/world/global-fund-results-report-2017

Gostin, Lawrence O., Oyewale Tomori, Suwit Wibulpolprasert, et al. 2016. 'Toward a common secure future: four global commissions in the wake of Ebola', *PLoS Medicine* 13(5): e1002042.

Gould, Deborah B. 2009. *Moving Politics: Emotion and ACT UP's Fight against AIDS*. Chicago, IL: University of Chicago Press.

Guernica. 2006. 'Share the wealth, or share the poverty'. Available at: https://www.guernicamag.com/either_share_the_wealth/

Hajer, Maarten A. 2003. 'A frame in the fields: policymaking and the reinvention of politics', in Maarten A. Hajer and Hendrik Wagenaar (eds.), *Deliberative Policy Analysis: Understanding Governance in the Network Society*. Cambridge: Cambridge University Press.

Hansen, Lena. 2012. 'Reconstructing desecuritisation: the normative-political in the Copenhagen School and directions for how to apply it', *Review of International Studies* 38(3): 535–46.

Harmon, Katherine. 2011. 'What will the next influenza pandemic look like?', *Scientific American*, 19 September. Available at: https://www.scientificamerican.com/article/next-influenza-pandemic/

Harris, Sheldon H. 2002. *Factories of Death: Japanese Biological Warfare, 1932–1945, and the American Cover-up*. New York: Routledge.

Hays, J.N. 2009. *The Burdens of Disease: Epidemic and Human Response in Western History*, rev. edn. New Brunswick, NJ: Rutgers University Press.

Henderson, Donald A., Thomas V. Inglesby, Jr., Tara O'Toole, Annie Fine and Marcelle Layton. 2001. 'Lessons from the West Nile viral encephalitis outbreak in New York City, 1999: implications for bioterrorism preparedness', *Clinical Infectious Diseases* 32(2): 277–82.

Herfst, Sander, E.J. Schrauwen, M. Linster, et al. 2012. 'Airborne transmission of influenza A/H5N1 virus between ferrets', *Science* 336(6088): 1534–41.

Heymann, David L. and Guénaël Rodier. 2004. 'Global surveillance, national surveillance, and SARS', *Emerging Infectious Diseases* 10(2): 173–5.

HM Government. 2008. *Health is Global: A UK Government Strategy 2008–13*. London: HMSO. Available at: http://webarchive.nationalarchives.gov.uk/20130105200335/http://www.dh.gov.uk/prod_consum_dh/groups/dh_digitalassets/@dh/@en/documents/digitalasset/dh_088753.pdf

HM Government. 2011. *Health is Global: An Outcomes Framework for Global Health 2011–2015*. London: HMSO. Available at https://www.gov.uk/government/uploads/system/uploads/attachment_data/file/67578/health-is-global.pdf

Hoffman, Steven J. 2010. 'The evolution, etiology and eventualities of the global health security regime', *Health Policy and Planning* 25: 510–22.

Hoffman, Steven J., Kevin Outterson, John-Arne Røttingen, et al. 2015. 'An international legal framework to address antimicrobial resistance', *Bulletin of the World Health Organization* 93: 66.

Holbrooke, Richard. 2006. Interview, PBS *Frontline*. Available from http://www.pbs.org/wgbh/pages/frontline/aids/interviews/holbrooke.html

Hooker, L. Claire, Christopher Mays, Chris Degeling, Gwendolyn L. Gilbert and Ian H. Kerridge. 2014. 'Don't be scared, be angry: the politics and ethics of Ebola', *Medical Journal of Australia* 201(6): 352–4.

Hoover, Herbert. 2011. *Freedom Betrayed: Herbert Hoover's Secret History of the Second World War and its Aftermath* (ed. George H. Nash). Stanford, CA: Hoover Institution Press.

Horton, Richard. 2013. 'Offline: is global health neo-colonialist?', *The Lancet* 382(9906): 1690.

Hotez, Peter J. 2008. *Forgotten People, Forgotten Diseases: The Neglected Tropical Diseases and Their Impact on Global Health and Development*. Washington, DC: American Society for Microbiology Press.

House Hansard. 2014. Questions without Notice. 27 October, p. 11985.

Howard-Jones, Norman. 1975. 'The scientific background of the International Sanitary Conferences, 1851–1938', *History of International Public Health, No.1*. Geneva: World Health Organization. Available at: http://apps.who.int/iris/bitstream/10665/62873/1/14549_eng.pdf

Huber, Valeska. 2006. 'The unification of the globe by disease? The International Sanitary Conferences on Cholera, 1851–1894', *The Historical Journal* 49(2): 453–76.

Imai, Masaki, Tokiko Watanabe, Masato Hatta, et al. 2012. 'Experimental adaptation of an influenza H5 HA confers respiratory droplet transmission to a reassortant H5 HA/H1N1 virus in ferrets', *Nature* 486: 420–8.

Ingram, Alan. 2008. 'Pandemic anxiety and global health security', in Rachel Pain and Susan J. Smith (eds.), *Fear: Critical Geopolitics and Everyday Life*. Aldershot: Ashgate.

Ingram, Alan. 2010. 'Governmentality and security in the US President's Emergency Plan for AIDS Relief (PEPFAR)', *GeoForum* 41(4): 607–16.

Ingram, Alan. 2011. 'The Pentagon's HIV/AIDS programmes: governmentality, political economy, security', *Geopolitics* 16(3): 655–74.

Jacobs, Lesley A. 2007. 'Rights and quarantine during the SARS global health crisis: differentiated legal consciousness in Hong Kong, Shanghai, and Toronto', *Law & Society Review* 41(3): 511–51.

Jain, Vageesh and Azeem Alam. 2017. 'Redefining universal health coverage in the age of global health security', *BMJ Global Health* 2(2): e000255.

Jefferson, Catherine, Filippa Lentzos and Claire Marris. 2014. 'Synthetic biology and biosecurity: challenging the "myths" ', *Frontiers in Public Health* 2: 115.

Jefferson, Tom, Mark Jones, Peter Doshi, et al. 2014. 'Neuramini-dase inhibitors for preventing and treating influenza in adults and children', *Cochrane Database of Systematic Reviews* 4: Art. No. CD008965.

Johnson, Creola. 1994. 'Quarantining HIV-infected Haitians: United States' violation of international law at Guantanamo Bay', *Howard Law Journal* 37(2): 305–31.

Kamradt-Scott, Adam. 2015. *Managing Global Health Security. The World Health Organization and Disease Outbreak Control.* Basingstoke: Palgrave Macmillan.

Kaplan, Robert L. 1994. 'The coming anarchy', *The Atlantic* 273(2): 44–77.

Keogh-Brown, Marcus R. and Richard D. Smith 2008. 'The economic impact of SARS: how does the reality match the predictions?', *Health Policy* 88(1): 110–20.

Kickbusch, Ilona. 2016. 'Politics or technocracy – what next for global health?', *International Journal of Health Policy and Management* 5(3): 201–4.

Kieny, Marie Paule and Delanyo Dovlo. 2015. 'Beyond Ebola: a new agenda for resilient health systems', *The Lancet* 385(9963): 91–2.

King, Mark S. 2014a. 'Remembering When the Band Played on and the Tragedy of Patient Zero', *Plus*, 8 May. Available at: https://www.hivplusmag.com/stigma/2014/05/08/remembering-when-band-played-and-tragedy-patient-zero

King, Mark S. 2014b. 'When People with HIV Became Suicide Bombers', MyFabulousDisease.com, 2 April. Available at: http://www.thebody.com/content/74248/when-people-with-hiv-became-suicide-bombers.html

Kluge, Hans, Jose Maria Martín-Moreno, Nedret Emiroglu, Guenael Rodier, Edward Kelley, Melitta Vujnovic and Govin Permanand. 2018. 'Strengthening global health security by embedding the International Health Regulations require-ments into national health systems', *BMJ Global Health* 3: e000656.

Koblentz, Gregory S. 2017. 'The *de novo* synthesis of horse-pox virus: implications for biosecurity and recommendations for preventing the reemergence of smallpox', *Health Security* 15(5): 1–9.

Kupferschmidt, Kai. 2017. 'How Canadian researchers recon-stituted an extinct poxvirus for $100,000 using mail-order

DNA', *Science*, 6 July. Available at: http://www.sciencemag.org/news/2017/07/how-canadian-researchers-reconstituted-extinct-poxvirus-100000-using-mail-order-dna

Labonté, Ronald, Ted Schrecker and Amit Sen Gupta. 2005. *Health for Some: Death, Disease and Disparity in a Globalizing Era*. Toronto: CSJ Research and Education.

Lakoff, Andrew. 2010. 'Two regimes of global health', *Humanity* 1(1): 59–79.

Lakoff, Andrew and Stephen J. Collier. 2008. 'The problem of securing health', in Andrew Lakoff and Stephen J. Collier (eds.), *Biosecurity Interventions: Global Health and Security in Question*. New York: Columbia University Press.

Landrain, Thomas, Morgan Meyer, Ariel Martin Perez and Remi Sussan. 2013. 'Do-it-yourself biology: challenges and promises for an open science and technology movement', *Systems and Synthetic Biology* 7: 115–26.

Laqueur, Walter. 1999. *The New Terrorism: Fanaticism and the Arms of Mass Destruction*. Oxford: Oxford University Press.

Lederberg, Joshua and Stanley C. Oaks (eds.). 1992. *Emerging Infections: Microbial Threats to Health in the United States*. Washington, DC: Institute of Medicine/National Academies Press.

Ledford, Heidi. 2015. 'CRISPR, the disruptor', *Nature* 532: 20–4.

Lee, Kelley and Colin McInnes. 2003. '*Health, foreign policy and security: a discussion paper*'. London: Nuffield Trust. Available at: https://www.nuffieldtrust.org.uk/files/2017-01/health-foreign-policy-and-security-discussion-web-final.pdf

Lee, Kelley and Colin McInnes. 2004. 'A conceptual framework for research and policy', in Alan Ingram (ed.), *Health, Foreign Policy & Security: Towards a Conceptual Framework for Research and Policy*. London: Nuffield Trust.

Leitenberg, Milton and Raymond A. Zilinskas. 2012. *The Soviet Biological Weapons Programme*. Cambridge, MA: Harvard University Press.

Lui, Andrew. 2012. *Why Canada Cares: Human Rights and Foreign Policy in Theory and Practice*. Kingston, Ontario: McGill-Queen's Press.

MacDougall, Clair. 2014. 'Liberian government's blunders pile up in the grip of Ebola', *Time*, 2 September. Available at: http://time.com/3247089/liberia-west-point-quarantine-monrovia/

MacFarlane, S. Neil and Yuen Foong Khong 2006. *Human Security and the UN: A Critical History*. Bloomington, IN: Indiana University Press.

Maclean, Ruth. 2016. 'Giving birth in Guinea: a life or death lottery bereft of midwives and medicine', *The Guardian*, 30 August. Available at: https://www.theguardian.com/global-development/2016/aug/29/giving-birth-guinea-maternal-health-life-death-lottery-bereft-midwives-medicine

Mahto, M., K. Ponnusamy, M. Schuhwerk, et al. 2006. 'Knowledge, attitudes and health outcomes in HIV-infected travellers to the USA', *HIV Medicine* 7(4): 201–4.

Malakoff, David. 2002. 'Pentagon proposal worries researchers', *Science* 296: 826.

Mann, Jonathan. 1988. *'The global picture of AIDS: address to the IV International Conference on AIDS, Stockholm, Sweden'*. Geneva: WHO.

Markel, Howard, Lawrence O. Gostin and David P. Fidler. 2007. 'Extensively drug-resistant tuberculosis: an isolation order, public health powers, and a global crisis', *Journal of the American Medical Association* 298(1): 83–6.

Mbali, Mandisa. 2013. *South African AIDS Activism and Global Health Politics*. Basingstoke: Palgrave Macmillan.

McInnes, Colin. 2005. *Health, Security and the Risk Society*. London: Nuffield Trust.

McInnes, Colin. 2016. 'Crisis! What Crisis? Global health and the 2014–15 West African Ebola outbreak', *Third World Quarterly* 37(3): 380–400.

McInnes, Colin and Kelley Lee. 2012. *Global Health and International Relations*. Cambridge: Polity.

McInnes, Colin and Anne Roemer-Mahler. 2017. 'From security to risk: reframing global health threats', *International Affairs* 93(6): 1313–37.

McInnes, Colin and Simon Rushton. 2010. 'HIV, AIDS and security: where are we now?', *International Affairs* 86(1): 225–45.

McInnes, Colin and Simon Rushton. 2013. 'HIV/AIDS and securitization theory', *European Journal of International Relations* 19(1): 115–38.

McKinlay, Alan. 2009. 'Foucault, plague, Defoe', *Culture and Organization* 15(2): 167–84.

McLeod, Kari S. 2000. 'Our sense of Snow: the myth of John Snow in medical geography', *Social Science & Medicine* 50(7–8): 923–35.

McMurray, Christine and Roy Smith. 2001. *Diseases of Globalization: Socioeconomic Transitions and Health*. London: Earthscan.

Miller, S.A. 2014. 'A top health expert warns against closing borders to stop Ebola', *Washington Times*, 6 October. Available at: http://www.washingtontimes.com/news/2014/oct/6/a-top-health-expert-warns-against-closing-borders-/

Moon, Suerie, Devi Sridhar, Muhammad A. Pate, et al. 2015. 'Will Ebola change the game? Ten essential reforms before the next pandemic. The report of the Harvard-LSHTM Independent Panel on the Global Response to Ebola', *The Lancet* 386(10009): 2204–21.

National Research Council. 2011. *Review of the Scientific Approaches Used during the FBI's Investigation of the 2001 Anthrax Letters*. Washington, DC: National Academies Press.

Nattrass, Nicoli and Gregg Gonsalves. 2009. 'Economics and the backlash against AIDS-specific funding'. CSSR Working Paper No. 254. Available at http://www.math.uct.ac.za/sites/default/files/image_tool/images/256/files/pubs/WP254.pdf

Nature. 2013. 'The DIY dilemma: misconceptions about do-it-yourself biology mean that opportunities are being missed', *Nature* 503 (26 November): 437–8.

Nelson, Christopher, Nicole Lurie, Jeffrey Wasserman, et al. 2007. 'Conceptualizing and defining public health emergency preparedness', *American Journal of Public Health* 97(Suppl 1): S9–11.

Ní Chonghaile, Clár. 2014. 'How Ebola turned a Guinean family tragedy into a west African crisis', *The Guardian*, 9 October. Available at: https://www.theguardian.com/global-development/2014/oct/09/ebola-guinea-family-west-africa-crisis

NIC (National Intelligence Council). 2000. The Global Infectious Disease Threat and Its Implications for the United States. NIE 99-17D, NIC. Available at: https://www.dni.gov/files/documents/infectiousdiseases_2000.pdf

Nixdorff, Kathryn. 2013. 'Education for life scientists on the dual-use implications of their research', *Science and Engineering Ethics* 19(5): 1487–90.

Noble, Ronald K. 2013. 'Keeping science in the right hands: policing the new biological frontier', *Foreign Affairs* 92 (November/December): 47–53.

Nowak, Rachel. 2001. 'Killer mousepox virus raises bioterror fears', *New Scientist*, 10 January. Available at: https://www.newscientist.com/article/dn311-killer-mousepox-virus-raises-bioterror-fears/

NSABB (National Science Advisory Board for Biosecurity). 2010. Addressing Biosecurity Concerns Related to Synthetic Biology. Available at: https://osp.od.nih.gov/wp-content/uploads/NSABB_SynBio_DRAFT_Report-FINAL-2_6-7-10.pdf

NSABB (National Science Advisory Board for Biosecurity). 2011. Strategies to Educate Amateur Biologists and Scientists in Non-life Science Disciplines About Dual Use Research in the Life Sciences. Available at: https://osp.od.nih.gov/wp-content/uploads/2013/06/FinalNSABBReport-AmateurBiologist-NonlifeScientists_June-2011_0.pdf

Nunes, João. 2014. *Security, Emancipation and the Politics of Health: A New Theoretical Perspective*. Abingdon: Routledge.

Nursing and Midwifery Council. 2016. 'NMC statement on the outcome of nurse Pauline Cafferkey's fitness to practise hearing'. 14 September. Available at: https://www.nmc.org.uk/news/news-and-updates/nmc-statement-on-the-outcome-of-nurse-pauline-cafferkeys-fitness-to-practise-hearing/

Nyman, Jonna. 2016. 'What is the value of security? Contextualising the negative/positive debate', *Review of International Studies* 42(5): 821–39.

Obama, Barack. 2014a. Speech to the United Nations Security Council, 25 September. Transcript available at: http://www.independent.co.uk/news/world/americas/ebola-virus-the-transcript-of-barack-obamas-speech-to-the-un-9756272.html

Obama, Barack. 2014b. *Remarks by the President on the Ebola Outbreak*. Centers for Disease Control and Prevention, Atlanta, Georgia, 16 September. Available at: https://www.whitehouse.gov/the-press-office/2014/09/16/remarks-president-ebola-outbreak

Obama, Barack. 2014c. 'Executive Order – Combating antibiotic-resistant bacteria', 18 September. Available at: https://www.whitehouse.gov/the-press-office/2014/09/18/executive-order-combating-antibiotic-resistant-bacteria

OHCHR (Office of the High Commissioner for Human Rights). 2008. *The Right to Health*. Fact Sheet No. 31. Geneva: OHCHR.

Available at: https://www.ohchr.org/Documents/Publications/
Factsheet31.pdf

Onishi, Norimtsu and Marc Santora. 2014. 'Ebola patient
in Dallas lied on screening form, Liberian airport official
says', *The New York Times*, 2 October. Available at: https://
www.nytimes.com/2014/10/03/world/africa/dallas-ebola-patient-
thomas-duncan-airport-screening.html

Ooms, Gorik. 2016. 'Navigating between stealth advocacy and
unconscious dogmatism: the challenge of researching the norms,
politics and power of global health', *International Journal of
Health Policy and Management* 4(10): 641–4.

Ooms, Gorik, Claudia Beiersmann, Walter Flores, et al. 2017.
'Synergies and tensions between universal health coverage
and global health security: why we need a second "Maximizing Positive Synergies" initiative', *BMJ Global Health* 2(1):
e000217.

Osterholm, M.T. and Olshaker, M. 2017. *Deadliest Enemy: Our
War Against Killer Germs*. Boston, MA: Little, Brown.

PAHO/WHO. 2017. Epidemiological Update: Cholera, 28 December.
Available at: https://www.paho.org/hq/index.php?option=com_
content&view=article&id=14038:28-december-2017-cholera-epi
demiological-update&Itemid=42346&lang=en

Paneth, Nigel. 2004. 'Assessing the contributions of John Snow
to epidemiology: 150 years after removal of the Broad Street
pump handle', *Epidemiology* 15(5): 514–16.

Parker, Laura. 2015. 'The anti-vaccine generation: how movement against shots got its start', *National Geographic*, 6
February. Available at: https://news.nationalgeographic.com/
news/2015/02/150206-measles-vaccine-disney-outbreak-polio-
health-science-infocus/

Parkhurst, Justin. 2017. *The Politics of Evidence: From Evidence-
Based Policy to the Good Governance of Evidence*. Abingdon:
Routledge.

Parliamentary Assembly of the Council of Europe. 2010. 'The
handling of the H1N1 pandemic: more transparency needed'.
Report: Social Health and Family Affairs Committee. Available at: http://assembly.coe.int/committeedocs/2010/20100604_
h1n1pandemic_e.pdf

Parmet, Wendy E. 2007. 'Legal power and legal rights – isolation
and quarantine in the case of drug-resistant tuberculosis', *New
England Journal of Medicine* 357(5): 433–5.

Pattani, Reena. 2015. 'Unsanctioned travel restrictions related to Ebola unravel the global social contract', *Canadian Medical Association Journal* 187(3): 166–7.

Patz, Jonathan A., Paul R. Epstein, Thomas A. Burke and John M. Balbus. 1996. 'Global climate change and emerging infectious diseases', *Journal of the American Medical Association* 275(3): 217–23.

Peckham, Robert. 2018. 'Polio, terror and the immunological worldview', *Global Public Health* 13(2): 189–210.

Pellecchia, Umberto, Rosa Crestani, Tom Decroo, Rafael Van den Bergh and Yasmine Al-Kourdi. 2015. 'Social consequences of Ebola containment measures in Liberia', *PLOS One* 10(12): e0143036.

PEPFAR. 2016. 'PEPFAR funding'. Available at: https://www. pepfar.gov/documents/organization/252516.pdf

Petro, James B. 2004. 'Intelligence support to the life science community: mitigating threats from bioterrorism', *Studies in Intelligence* 48(3): 57–68.

Piot, Peter. 2012. *No Time to Lose: A Life in Pursuit of Deadly Viruses*. New York: W.W. Norton.

Pisani, Elizabeth. 2008. *The Wisdom of Whores: Bureaucrats, Brothels and the Business of AIDS*. London: Granta.

Porta, Miquel. 2014. *A Dictionary of Epidemiology*. Oxford: Oxford University Press.

Price-Smith, Andrew T. 2001. *The Health of Nations: Infectious Disease, Environmental Change, and their Effects on National Security and Development*. Cambridge, MA: MIT Press.

Price-Smith, Andrew T. 2009. *Contagion and Chaos: Disease, Ecology and National Security in the Era of Globalization*. Cambridge, MA: MIT Press.

Price-Smith, Andrew and Jackson Porreca. 2016. 'Fear, apathy, and the Ebola crisis (2014–15): psychology and problems of global health governance', *Global Health Governance* X(1): 18–34.

Quereshi, Sarah N. 1995. 'Global ostracism of HIV-positive aliens: international restrictions barring HIV-positive aliens', *Maryland Journal of International Law and Trade* 19: 81–120.

Ratner, Judith. 2003. 'The legacy of Guantánamo', *The Nation*, 14 July. Available at: https://www.thenation.com/article/ legacy-guantanamo/

Regalado, Antonio. 2016. 'Rewriting life: top U.S. intelligence official calls gene editing a WMD threat', *MIT Technology*

Review. Available at: https://www.technologyreview.com/s/600774/top-us-intelligence-official-calls-gene-editing-a-wmd-threat/

Reinarman, Craig and Harry G. Levine. 1989. 'Crack in context: politics and media in the shaping of a drug scare', *Contemporary Drug Problems* 16: 535–77.

Reppy, Judith. 2008. 'A biomedical military–industrial complex?', *Technovation* 28(12): 802–11.

Reuters. 2016. 'Ivory Coast re-opens western borders closed during Ebola epidemic', 9 September. Available at: http://news.trust.org/item/20160909103921-1jmqw/

Review Committee on the Role of the International Health Regulations (2005) in the Ebola Outbreak and Response. 2016. 'Implementation of the International Health Regulations (2005)', A69/21, 13 May. Available at: http://apps.who.int/gb/ebwha/pdf_files/WHA69/A69_21-en.pdf?ua=1

Revill, James, M. Daniela Candia Carnevali, Åke Forsberg, Anna Holmström, Johannes Rath, Zabta Khan Shinwari and Giulio M. Mancini. 2012. 'Lessons learned from implementing education on dual use in Austria, Italy, Pakistan and Sweden', *Medicine, Conflict and Survival* 28(1): 31–44.

Rodier, Guénaël, Allison L. Greenspan, James M. Hughes and David L. Heymann. 2007. 'Global public health security', *Emerging Infectious Diseases* 13(10): 1447–52.

Rushton, Simon. 2010. 'AIDS and international security in the United Nations system', *Health Policy and Planning* 25(6): 495–504.

Rushton, Simon. 2011. 'Global health security: Security for whom? Security from what?', *Political Studies* 59(4): 779–96.

Rushton, Simon. 2012. 'The global debate over HIV-related travel restrictions: framing and policy change'. *Global Public Health* 7(Supp.2): S159–S175.

Rushton, Simon. 2015. 'The politics of researching global health politics', *International Journal of Health Policy and Management* 4(5): 311–14.

Saéz, Almudena Marí, Sabrina Weiss, Kathrin Nowak, et al. 2014. 'Investigating the zoonotic origin of the West African Ebola epidemic', *EMBO Molecular Medicine* 7(1): 17–23.

Schabas, Richard. 2004. 'Severe acute respiratory syndrome: did quarantine help?', *Canadian Journal of Infectious Diseases and Medical Microbiology* 15(4): 204.

Schlesinger, Mark. 2002. 'A loss of faith: the sources of reduced political legitimacy for the American medical profession', *The Millbank Quarterly* 80(2): 185–235.

Schrecker, Ted and Clare Bambra. 2015. *How Politics Makes Us Sick: Neoliberal Epidemics*. Basingstoke: Palgrave Macmillan.

Schwartz, Robert and Bruce Rosen. 2004. 'The politics of evidence-based health policy-making', *Public Money & Management* 24(2): 121–7.

Scientists Working Group on Biological and Chemical Weapons. 2010. 'Biological threats: a matter of balance', *Bulletin of the Atomic Scientists*, 2 February.

Selgelid, Michael J. 2008. 'Governance of dual-use research: an ethical dilemma', *Bulletin of the World Health Organization* 87: 720–3.

Selgelid, Michael J. and Lorna Weir. 2010. 'The mousepox experience: an interview with Ronald Jackson and Ian Ramshaw on dual-use research', *EMBO Reports* 11(1): 18–24.

Senate Hansard. 2014. 'Matters of urgency', 29 October, p. 8174.

Shiffman, Jeremy, David Berlan and Tamara Hafner. 2009. 'Has aid for AIDS raised all health funding boats?', *JAIDS* 52(Supp 1): S45–8.

Shilts, Randy. 1987. *And The Band Played On: Politics, People and the AIDS Epidemic*. New York: St Martin's Press.

Shilts, Randy. 2007. *And The Band Played On: Politics, People and the AIDS Epidemic* (rev. edn). New York: St. Martin's Griffin.

Shooter, R.A. 1980. *Report of the Investigation into the Cause of the 1978 Birmingham Smallpox Occurrence*. London: HMSO.

Shute, Joe. 2014. 'Ebola: inside Liberia's West Point slum', *The Telegraph*, 16 December. Available at: https://www.telegraph.co.uk/news/worldnews/ebola/11295271/Ebola-inside-Liberias-West-Point-slum.html

Sjöstedt, Roxanna. 2008. 'Exploring the construction of threats: the securitization of HIV/AIDS in Russia', *Security Dialogue* 39(1): 7–29.

Smith, Alex Duval. 2009. 'Experts want African aid funds channelled away from HIV', *The Guardian*, 25 October. Available at: https://www.theguardian.com/world/2009/oct/25/aids-hiv-africa-aid-scientists

Sontag, Susan. 1989. *AIDS and its Metaphors*. London: Allen Lane.

Spellberg, Brad and Bonnie Taylor-Blake. 2013. 'On the exoneration of Dr. William H. Stewart: debunking an urban legend', *Infectious Diseases of Poverty* 2(3): 1–5.

Spottiswoode, Roger (Dir.). 1993. *And The Band Played On* (HBO Films).

Stewart, Kirsty. 2016. 'Ebola nurse Pauline Cafferkey "concealed her high temperature from medics after returning from Sierra Leone" ', *Daily Mirror*, 18 August. Available at: https://www.mirror.co.uk/news/uk-news/ebola-nurse-pauline-cafferkey-concealed-8656055

Sun, Lena H. 2018. 'Inside the secret US stockpile meant to save us all in a bioterror attack', *The Washington Post*, 24 April. Available at: https://www.washingtonpost.com/news/to-your-health/wp/2018/04/24/inside-the-secret-u-s-stockpile-meant-to-save-us-all-in-a-bioterror-attack/?noredirect=on&utm_term=.35c85a938b9e

Théiren, Jean-Philippe. 2012. 'Human security: the making of a UN ideology', *Global Society* 26(2): 191–213.

Thomas, Anne-Claire, Tharcisse Nkunzimana, Ana Perez Hoyos and François Kayitakire. 2014. 'Impact of the West African Ebola virus disease outbreak on food security'. *JRC Science and Policy Reports, December*. Brussels: European Commission Joint Research Centre.

Toebes, Birgit. 2015. 'Human rights and public health: towards a balanced relationship', *The International Journal of Human Rights* 19(4): 488–504.

Tognotti, Eugenia. 2013. 'Lessons from the history of quarantine, from plague to influenza A', *Emerging Infectious Diseases* 19(2): 254–9.

Treatment Action Campaign. 2009. 'A response to Roger England'. Available at: https://tac.org.za/news/a-response-to-roger-england/

Tulman, E.R., G. Delhon, C.L. Afonso, et al. 2006. 'Genome of horsepox virus', *Journal of Virology* 80(18): 9244–58.

UNAIDS. 2000. *Report on the Global HIV/AIDS Epidemic, June 2000*. Geneva: UNAIDS. Available at http://data.unaids.org/pub/report/2000/2000_gr_en.pdf

UNDP. 1994. *Human Development Report 1994*. New York: UNDP.

UNDP. 2016. *Human Development Report 2016*. New York: UNDP. Available at: http://hdr.undp.org/en/2016-report

UNICEF. 2018. Trends in estimates of maternal mortality ratio (MMR; maternal deaths per 100,000 live births)

1990–2015. Data available at: https://data.unicef.org/wp-content/uploads/2015/12/MMR_Matdeaths_LTR-trend-estimates-1990-2015_MMEIG.xlsx

United Nations. 2001. 'Declaration of Commitment First Global "Battle Plan" Against AIDS, General Assembly President Tells Special Session'. GA/SM/264 (27 June). Available at: http://www.un.org/News/Press/docs/2001/gasm264.doc.htm

United Nations. 2015. *The Millennium Development Goals Report 2015*. New York: UN. Available at: https://unstats.un.org/unsd/mdg/Resources/Static/Products/Progress2015/English2015.pdf

United Nations Security Council. 2014. S/RES/2177 (18 September).

United Nations Trust Fund for Human Security. 2018. 'Agenda 2030'. Available at: https://www.un.org/humansecurity/agenda-2030/

UN News. 2017. 'Human security approach "central" to achieving sustainable development – UN officials', 7 July. Available at: https://news.un.org/en/story/2017/07/561142-human-security-approach-central-achieving-sustainable-development-un-officials

US Department of Justice. 2010. Amerithrax Investigative Summary, 19 February. Available at: http://www.justice.gov/archive/amerithrax/docs/amx-investigative-summary.pdf

van Noorden, Richard. 2014. 'Report disputes benefit of stockpiling Tamiflu', *Nature*. doi:10.1038/nature.2014.15022.

Verweij, Marcel and Angus Dawson. 2010. 'Shutting up infected houses: infectious disease control, past and present', *Public Health Ethics* 3(1): 1–3.

Vogel, Kathleen M. 2013. 'Intelligent assessment: putting emerging biotechnology threats in context', *Bulletin of the Atomic Scientists* 69(1): 43–52.

Vogel, Kathleen M. 2014. 'Revolution versus evolution?: Understanding scientific and technological diffusion in synthetic biology and their implications for biosecurity policies', *BioSocieties* 9(4): 365–92.

Wagenaar, Bradley H., Orvalho Augusto, Jason Beste, et al. 2018. 'The 2014–2015 Ebola virus disease outbreak and primary healthcare delivery in Liberia: Time-series analyses for 2010–2016', *PLoS Medicine* 15(2): e1002508.

Wald, Priscilla. 2008. *Contagious: Cultures, Carriers, and the Outbreak Narrative*. Durham, NC: Duke University Press.

Warner-Smith, Matthew, Deborah Rugg, Luisa Frescura and Saba Moussavi. 2009. 'Monitoring the 2001 Declaration of

Commitment on HIV/AIDS', *JAIDS – Journal of Acquired Immune Deficiency Syndromes* 52(Supp. 2): S77–S86.

Watson, James L. 2006. 'SARS and the consequences for globalization', in Arthur Kleinman and James L. Watson (eds.), *SARS in China: Prelude to Pandemic?* Stanford, CA: Stanford University Press, pp. 196–204.

Watts, Nick, W. Neil Adger, Paolo Agnolucci, et al. 2015. 'Health and climate change: policy responses to protect public health', *The Lancet* 386: 1861–914.

WEF (World Economic Forum). 2017. *The Global Risks Report 2017, 12th Edition.* Geneva: WEF. Available at: http://www3.weforum.org/docs/GRR17_Report_web.pdf

Weir, Lorna and Eric Mykhalovskiy. 2010. *Global Public Health Vigilance: Creating a World on Alert.* New York: Routledge.

WHA. 1951. *International Sanitary Regulations, adopted by the World Health Assembly on 25 May 1951.* Geneva: WHO.

WHA. 1980. 'Declaration of the global eradication of Smallpox'. WHA33.3, 8 May. Available at: http://apps.who.int/iris/bitstream/10665/155528/1/WHA33_R3_eng.pdf

WHA. 2001. 'Global health security – epidemic alert and response'. WHA51.14, 21 May. Available at: http://apps.who.int/medicinedocs/documents/s16356e/s16356e.pdf

WHA. 2015. 'WHA68(10): 2014 Ebola virus disease outbreak and follow-up to the Special Session of the Executive Board on Ebola', A68/DIV./3. Available at: http://apps.who.int/gb/ebwha/pdf_files/WHA68/A68_DIV3-en.pdf?ua=1

White House. 1996. Presidential Decision Directive NSTC-7. Available at: https://fas.org/irp/offdocs/pdd/pdd-nstc-7.pdf

WHO. 2001. 'Global health security – epidemic alert and response'. A/54/9, 2 April. Available at: http://apps.who.int/medicinedocs/documents/s16357e/s16357e.pdf

WHO. 2003. 'Summary of probable SARS cases with onset of illness from 1 November 2002 to 31 July 2003 (based on data as of 31 December 2003)'. Available at: http://www.who.int/csr/sars/country/table2004_04_21/en/.

WHO. 2006. *'Biorisk management: laboratory biosecurity guidance, September 2006'.* Geneva: WHO.

WHO. 2007. *The World Health Report 2007. A Safer Future: Global Public Health Security in the 21st Century.* Geneva: WHO. Available at: http://www.who.int/whr/2007/whr07_en.pdf

WHO. 2009. *Pandemic Influenza Preparedness and Response: A Guidance Document*. Geneva: WHO. Available at: http://apps.who.int/iris/bitstream/10665/44123/1/9789241547680_eng.pdf

WHO. 2010. 'The international response to the influenza pandemic: WHO responds to the critics'. Pandemic (H1N1) 2009 briefing note 21, 10 June. Available at: http://www.who.int/csr/disease/swineflu/notes/briefing_20100610/en/

WHO. 2013. *Checklist and Indicators for Monitoring Progress in the Development of IHR Core Capacities in States Parties*. Geneva: WHO. Available at: http://apps.who.int/iris/bitstream/handle/10665/84933/WHO_HSE_GCR_2013.2_eng.pdf;jsessionid=F4D00E032D38D58E6D88E84D8A04F3AC?sequence=1

WHO. 2014a. *Interim Guidance: Ebola Event Management at Points of Entry, September 2014*. Geneva: WHO. Available at: http://apps.who.int/iris/bitstream/10665/131827/1/WHO_EVD_Guidance_PoE_14.1_eng.pdf

WHO. 2014b. 'Antimicrobial resistance'. Fact sheet no. 194. Available at: http://www.who.int/mediacentre/factsheets/fs194/en/

WHO. 2015. 'International Health Regulations: Global Outbreak Alert and Response Network (GOARN)'. Available at: http://www.who.int/ihr/about/IHR_Global_Outbreak_Alert_and_Response_Network_respond.pdf?ua=1

WHO. 2016. *International Health Regulations (2005), Third Edition*. Geneva: WHO. Available at: http://apps.who.int/iris/bitstream/10665/246107/1/9789241580496-eng.pdf?ua=1

WHO. 2017. International Health Regulations Monitoring Framework: Implementation status of core capacity requirements 2010–2017. Average of 13 core capacity scores: 2017. Available at: http://gamapserver.who.int/gho/interactive_charts/ihr/monitoring/atlas.html

WHO. 2018a. Contingency Fund for Emergencies (CFE). Available at http://www.who.int/emergencies/funding/contingency-fund/en/

WHO. 2018b. 'The top 10 causes of death'. Available at: http://www.who.int/news-room/fact-sheets/detail/the-top-10-causes-of-death

Woodling, Marie, Owain David Williams and Simon Rushton. 2012. 'New life in old frames: HIV, development and the "AIDS plus MDGs" approach', *Global Public Health* 7(Supp. 2): S144–58.

World Bank. 2018. 'WHO and World Bank group join forces to strengthen global health security'. Press release, 24 May. Available at: http://www.worldbank.org/en/news/press-release/2018/05/24/who-and-world-bank-group-join-forces-to-strengthen-global-health-security

World Food Programme. 2014. 'West and Central Africa markets update: special issue on the Ebola outbreak – 29 September 2014', Special Bulletin No. 3, September. Available at: http://documents.wfp.org/stellent/groups/public/documents/ena/wfp268458.pdf?_ga=2.117690121.1261128345.1498653090-2029103948.1479737297

Worobey, Michael, Thomas D. Watts, Richard A. McKay, et al. 2016. '1970s and "Patient 0" HIV-1 genomes illuminate early HIV/AIDS history in North America', *Nature* 539(7627): 98–101.

Worsnop, Catherine. 2017. 'Domestic politics and the WHO's International Health Regulations: explaining the use of trade and travel barriers during disease outbreaks', *The Review of International Organizations* 12(3): 365–95.

Youde, Jeremy. 2012. *Global Health Governance*. Cambridge: Polity.

Zidar, Andraž. 2015. 'WHO International Health Regulations and human rights: from allusion to inclusion', *The International Journal of Human Rights* 19(4): 505–26.

Index